TWO TIMER

Janie Williams Rouse

Two Timer

Copyright © 2022 Janie Williams Rouse

ISBN: 978-0-578-36420-9

Printed in the United States of America

Introduction

This is a message of gratefulness and miracles. Our Lord and Savior granted these and much more. His grace and mercy have kept me all this time. Looking back, it seemed undeserving, but who am I to question His judgment? There were many times His presence was felt. There are two times that stand out when He spoke in a loud voice.

This is for all the people that kept telling me to write it down! After reading this, if someone is inspired to keep moving forward with positive energy, the purpose is fulfilled. Some will just laugh at the funny parts of the story, if so, then mission accomplished. Some might be inspired to share their own story. Once again, mission accomplished. I believe God has a wonderful sense of humor too. He made us.

An excellent place to start is at the beginning. The earliest memories are of my brothers and sisters helping Mama takecare of us. A lot of attention was given to me being the babyat home. Someone was always making sure there was no love lacking for me. There were brothers and sisters old enough to have been my parents. There were ten children in our house and our Mama and Daddy. That amounts to twelve people in a tiny little house in the woods.

Each child was no more than sixteen months apart, even when Mama lost or miscarried a baby. Mama must have been so tired. My only memory of Mama is her reaching down to pick me up, and her hair would fall in my face. My siblings did everything to entertain my next older brother and me. I was three, so he was almost five. The older girls tried to keep me pristine and tidy. I suppose the frustrations I caused outdid them. I wanted to be outside with the boys climbing trees, running, yelling, and fighting. Playing ball was considered a game for boys. It looked like so much fun. I wanted to play with them.

My sisters wanted to keep me in the house or play nicely outside with dolls and such. The mulberry patch right next to the house looked mysterious. All the older children would pick berries quite often. The patch seemed very big to me. The mulberry bushes were so dense a person could not stand outside the patch and see inside. One could see only one of the picker's heads bobbing up and down to get the berries. Mulberry bushes have thin, extremely sharp thorns. The berries were so sweet once they turned the deep purple color. Going into the patch meant eating as you picked. Certain snakes also loved the mulberries and never ceased to feast on them. My older siblings often went in to pick the berries and left the smaller children on the patch's edges. The moment the others were busy picking berries, I would sneak into the patch with them. It seems as soon as I got a big juicy berry, someone would yell, "snake!" I would be snatched up and taken out of the berry patch to sit on the edge and watch them pick and eat juicy berries. Mama would make a mulberry "doobie." A doobie is just like a peach cobbler but with mulberries instead of peaches. The saying was this berry pie "do be good." That is how it got the name. The thought of a sweet treat was happiness for a little child. The smell of the doobie baking made the mouth water for a sweet taste.

Sometime later, conversations were overheard about the baby that was coming. At three years old, I was the baby and could not understand where "the baby" was coming from! Soon after, Cousin Ella came over. Later that evening, the older children gathered us into the bedroom to wait. There was no television or radio, so we huddled together, just waiting, constantly told to be quiet. It seemed much later that we heard a loud scream, a baby crying, and much more screaming.

Cousin Ella came to the door and whispered something. The older children started crying and wailing. Later, we were told that Mama had died. I was being squeezed so tight that it hurt. Sometime later, I was told that we had a baby brother. He had been taken by an older couple that was relatives. Nobody got to see him or hold him except maybe some of the older children. My new brother Arthur (Hercules) would not meet Ben and me until he was three years old.

Herc looked just like me, and I looked just like Daddy. I was still the baby in the house because the new baby was being taken care of someplace else.

Mama dying made Daddy drink more and more. Daddy worked hard and drank hard. There were ten children at home to clothe and feed and a newborn baby to check on. Daddy cut cross ties for a living. This is called pulpwood. This kind of work was extremely hard, and Daddy worked from sunup to sundown Monday through Friday every week.

Daddy would come in from work so dirty and so tired. Most days, he would take a bath, eat and go to bed. Daddy would buy groceries on Saturdays. The grocery would come in cardboard boxes as he brought food for ten children and himself. Grits and meal came from the mill and was in cloth bags. Unloading the bags would cause a cloud of dust to settle slowly. Lots of time, the food would not last the entire week. My sisters would stretch the little we had. It was not uncommon to eat a bowl of grits with a few fried okra on top. To get a small piece of fatback was special. Fatback is pork belly with a slim piece of red meat left attached. It could season soups or stand-in for bacon. Most meats were smoked and would last longer unrefrigerated. A lot of families did not have refrigerators. Chickens, turkeys, and sometimes ducks were usually raised in the yard a little way from the house. A mean rooster would be chicken and dumplings for dinner. This was the life for us after Mama died.

Daddy kept drinking more and more. Daddy was still a young man and desired the company of women. Mama, after all, was not coming back. Daddy had a daughter with his girlfriend. The young girl was just two years younger than our baby brother and lived not far from where he lived. These two got to know each other and grew up together, going to the same schools from elementary all the way through high school.

At the age of five, Aunt Thelma and Uncle Burton came to take me to their home in Florida. They were going to raise me as their own. Daddy agreed and then ran the car down, lifted me out, and insisted he could not let me go. There was a whole lot of crying by Aunt Thelma and cursing on the part of the men. Uncle Burton and his sisters never thought Daddy was a good husband for Mama. My feelings were mixed, not knowing what Florida was.

It seemed to be a place where rich people lived because Uncle Burton and Aunt Thelma always had money. Each time a box of sweet oranges was given to the family. Enough food to last a few days was always bought. The money was to buy treats for us at the little store down the road. Our favorite was the vanilla ice cream with the little wooden spoon attached. Surely these people were rich because each one of us got one of those ice cream cups everytime they visited! The ice cream cups were five cents each.

Any car coming down our little dirt road was exciting. Thatgreen Chevrolet Belair rolling up to our dirt yard was a tripto the store.

Some time passed before any attempt to get Ben and my next older brother to Florida to live with Uncle Burton and Aunt Thelma. I went to stay with my Aunt Felicia, who had a pomegranate tree right there at the edge of the back porch. There was one big fruit on the tree when I got there. Aunt Felicia said when it was time, I could have a piece. Auntie had two daughters and one son. The oldest girl was fifteen; the youngest was thirteen. The maturity levels seemed reversed, though. The youngest seemed more advanced than the oldest.

All the older boys in our family are called Bubba, so Auntie had a Bubba. I remember the treatment of Bubba was as though there was a shortcoming in his mental abilities.

He remains to this day one of the nicest people I have ever met. The oldest daughter resented my presence and would pinch or hit me every chance she got. That one felt that Auntie favored me.

Bubba treated me like the little five-year-old cousin his mother loved; therefore, he also loved me. During this time with Aunt Felicia and her family, the oldest girl had a baby. The girl was not mature or capable of taking care of a baby. Many years later, it dawned on me that mental illness was the reason for this inability to embrace motherhood. There were times my cousin would tell me to watch the baby and then just leave. Auntie would be at work, of course. Auntie would come home and ask, "Where is she?" The only thing I knew for sure was that my cousin had left, and I watched her walking down the road. Considering the times for people of color, healthcare was not available and too expensive.

The baby was a pretty little girl, that seemed really skinny. She was small as a baby doll. The mother resented having to take care of her baby. Auntie and Bubba would leave for work, and the youngest girl would leave for school. That left Reverend Green (who was blind), the baby, her mother, and me until Auntie came home. Trying to be invisible during this time was not hard because the mother and baby would stay in the bedroom most days. One day Auntie got home and went to check on the mother and baby and came out crying. There was a small, still little bundle in her arms. "Lawd, Lawd" is all that was said. Then later, a hole was dug at the back of the property, and the baby was laid to rest. There was a little wooden cross put there to mark the spot.

Shortly after that, daddy came for me to go stay with another Auntie who had eleven children of her own! My skin color and features were just like my Daddy. My Auntie and the children still at home were much lighter-skinned than me. There was no difference in the treatment received, no teasing from the other children. If anything, preferential treatment was the order of the day. The stay there would be shorter than the last. Daddy came for me, I am told, within one week. Daddy and this Auntie never got along.

The story is that Daddy refused to separate the two youngest children permanently. Daddy delivered me to my siblings and continued working to take care of us. The same pattern as before, work all week, drink on Fridays and bring groceries to us sometime on Saturday. By now, Daddy had a regular girlfriend who had several children. Throughout my lifetime, Daddy always kept a car. It was his pride and joy. He kept it spotless. The car would always have a shine. I never remember riding in the car with Daddy except when he took me from Uncle Burton and Aunt Thelma that day.

Daddy came rolling into the yard late one Saturday afternoon and yelled for my brothers to unload the car. All of us came running to see if perhaps there were some cookies or some small treat for us. It seemed that the lady Daddy was seeing had a lot of children. The children were eating ice cream in the back seat of Daddy's car.

The younger one was leaning out of the window sticking his tongue out, and eating a cup of ice cream. There was no treat for any of us, and so at five years old, I reached up and knocked his cup to the sand. He started screaming and calling me names, so I started cussing and hitting him. Daddy's girlfriend, his mother, started yelling for Daddy to come to get the little wild children and take her from there. My brothers came back to the car to unload the rest of our food right about this time. One of the larger children in the car said something, and then it was truly a battle. Daddy came outside laughing and trying to chastise me all at once. He got behind the wheel and drove away. He never brought that lady there to our house again. They had no business riding in my Daddy's good car and eating ice cream!

A while after this, Uncle Burton and Aunt Thelma came back. Whenever the green Chevrolet rolled into the yard, something good was about to happen. It never failed. This time the Auntie with the eleven children was with them. The grownups were talking quietly away from the children. A little later on, Aunt Thelma told Benjamin and me that we would be going to live with them in Florida. They were coming to pick us up the next day. I did not believe it. I had already started to Florida once before with them and ended up right back home.

My older sisters were washing my hair and straightening it. Our best clothes were cleaned in the tub. Later in the evening, we were both bathed in the same No. 3 tin tub. All of the sisters and brothers seemed happy that we were leaving. I wondered why they were happy that we would be gone from there, from them, which is all we ever knew.

In the early morning, the Chevrolet pulled up alongside the house. Aunt Thelma had new clothes for Benjamin and me to wear. Our sisters were told to get us dressed. Not too long after that, hugs were shared all around; we loaded into the car and started a new adventure.

* * *

We kept looking back until the curve in the road would not let us see the house or our brothers and sisters anymore. I cried. My brother thought that if I did not shut up, they were going to take us back. Benjamin, my brother, thought I was just dumb. He was older, almost eight, and I was almost six.

Inside that car, a whole new world started for my brother and me. The miles flew by as 17 South kept taking us farther and farther away. Aunt Thelma had some sweet cakes, fried chicken, and kool-aide in jars. It tasted so good. It was not hard to start calling Aunt Thelma Mama, but it was kind of strange to call Uncle Burton Daddy. You see, we still had our Daddy, but I never really remembered Mama.

There were only two stops made on that trip. One-stop was outside Brunswick, Georgia, almost at the Florida/Georgia state lines. Daddy knew a black man that had a gas station and a restaurant there that sat back from the road. They sold barbeque from a pit outback. This was a new experience. No black man near where our house was had a gas station and a restaurant with an indoor toilet. Back in the car again and on our way, I kept looking back at that place. I thought it would never be seen again.

In fact, every other summer during the trips back to South Carolina, this was always one of the rest and refuel stops. Once or twice over the years, lunch was had in a restaurant in downtown Savannah owned and operated by a cousin of my Uncle Burton. The place outside Brunswick,

GA, was a novelty for us, but the restaurant in Savannah was a dream. Each one of the tables had a tablecloth with a plastic flower in a vase. Somebody came to the table and asked our parents what we would like to order. There were other customers in the place, and it smelled so good in there. My brother and me had never been in or eaten in a restaurant before. We stared at everything and everyone until Mama (Aunt Thelma) told us it was impolite to stare.

The waitress brought our food on a big tray; Mama prayed, of course, then we ate our lunch. It was delicious.

Many summer trips were made back to South Carolina. There was only one other time we had lunch in Savannah. It was four or five years after moving to Florida. Each time the trip was made, I asked if lunch would be in Savannah. Daddy (Uncle Burton) seemed to get angry each time the question was asked. Daddy would drive right on through as if we had never stopped there at all. "We ain't stopping there!" he would yell. I knew to be quiet then.

The year was 1960, and there was a lot of unrest all over the United States. Years later, I found out that Daddy knew of some incident that had taken place in Savannah. The family was not going to stop anywhere that might put us in jeopardy. Highway 17 North used to go right through downtown Savannah. The Civil Rights Movement was in full momentum by this time. People of color were being attacked for no reason other than the fact that their skin color was different. There was going to be a long fight for equal treatment under the law. Mama and Daddy protected us from much of the horror of it all.

Daddy and Mama had made a promise to always keep my brother and me in touch with our siblings. From then on, we made the trip with no stop in Savannah. The fond memory of the time we had lunch is still quite clear. I smile, thinking of it. The other sure stop going North or South was a little town in Florida named Hastings.

Hastings was where Mama (Aunt Thelma) was from. It is outside of Palatka, Florida. The family here looked forward to the couple of hours we spent there on each trip. There were still a lot of draw bridges in operation. Most towns near or on the water had to have one. These draw bridges were usually lined with confederate soldiers. It was scary to wait for the bridge to open and close. One could see the water way down below. It seemed as if the car was slipping down as the waiting took place. I learned not to look down at that water.

The bridge in Palatka, FL was small compared to Jacksonville or Savannah. To a small child it seemed really large and very high up in the air. Daddy would fall asleep anywhere as he got older. One time as the trip was in progress, he dozed behind the wheel. He came awake fully just as the Palatka bridge was blinking the red light. This was the signal that the bridge was about to open. He stopped just in time. He did not drive to South Carolina again, and Mama never made the trip again. It was her last

Summer in South Carolina. Mama was sick a lot these days.

Daddy was around sixty- three or maybe sixty -four years old. I was fifteen years old. The next time he made the trip, I was nineteen, and I drove him in his brand-new Chevy pickup truck. It was white with a royal blue interior. By this time, the interstate road system had been in place for a while. He forbade me to get on the interstate. Knowing this would cut our drive time by at least three hours, I would jump on the interstate each time he fell asleep. Sixty miles an hour was the speed limit. The speed limit on 17North never went higher than 50 mph. Passing by Savannah, Daddy woke up. He told me to get back on Highway 17. I did what he told me to do, and it took us almost four more hours to get to Yemassee, SC! Mama was not feeling well, so she did not come along.

It was important that the family travel during the daytime. Everything revolved around getting to our destinations before dark. The next stop after Palatka was Oviedo. Everything was brand new to Ben and me. Pulling into the backyard of what looked like a big house, we just stared. Red bells were in bloom along the driveway like hedges. Unloading the car did not take too long. Mama cooked some pork and beans, sausage, and rice for supper. Then we took baths and went to bed in a small room up in the front of the house.

The good smell of ham cooking woke us up the next morning. There were also homemade biscuits. Mama filled our plates and told us that we would both be going to the doctor for a checkup on Monday morning. This was a Saturday morning. Mama had an endless list of things to do. Clothes to wash, Sunday dinner to prepare, and get all our stuff ready for church. The only time we had been to church was at the funeral service for our natural Mama.

Mama and Daddy had been away in South Carolina for five days. The male friend's Daddy had looking out for the place while they were gone came to welcome them back. They also wanted to see the two children brought back from South Carolina. People looked at us and would say, "They look like twins." Brothers and sisters often look alike. Mama told us Sunday School was the first thing in the morning, right after breakfast, then church.

Early the next morning, after breakfast, Mama started getting us ready. Daddy was the Superintendent of the Sunday School and had to be there first. The church was diagonal across the street from our house. It was a two-minute walk at the most. Sunday School was fascinating to attend. It was studying and learning the bible.

It would be the same regimen every Sunday. The only thing that changed was the age groups of the classes. Once a certain age was reached, a child moved to another higher age group. The only distinction between the adults was young adults and seniors. Each class would have a learning and discussion session, take up an offering then move to the center seating aisle to make the class report. There was always a forty-five-minute break between Sunday School and 11:00 A.M. Church Services.

The church would last at least three hours. It was quite difficult for a young boy and girl to sit still. It was even harder for those that had never spent time in any church service. Mama made us sit on the second pew at the front of the church. Sitting there, Daddy was to our immediate left in the deacon's corner. Mama sat on the right in the deaconess corner. Any movement at all could be seen from either direction. Any parent, usher, or grownup had the authority to chastise you. The best thing to do was follow the rules and pray the Pastor would wrap it up soon. That rarely happened in our church. There were two services on the second and fourth Sundays. First Sunday was deacon and missionary meetings held in the afternoons at the church. Baptist Young People's Union (BYPU) was every third Sunday afternoon.

The belief was to keep the children busy and involved, which would keep them out of trouble. Children in the church were either usher or sang with the junior choir. One could not participate in any of these activities if that person did not join the church. Mama said singing in the choir was not an option because the choir traveled sometimes. Mama was a senior usher. The ushers only traveled when the church had an engagement or the usher's union had meetings at other churches. Mama was not about to let her daughter go off without her.

My Mama, this good and perfect woman, was all I wanted to be. I joined the church at six years old and was baptized after a week of seeking. My brother joined that same day. Two other children along with my brother and me, were baptized the same day. Baptism was at Georgia Camp Lake. The entire body is taken under the water (held by deacons) and then brought back up. All sins were cleansed at this time. A big dinner celebration was then held. It was usually at the house of the mother of the Church. My Mama was the mother of the Church when I was baptized. The big dinner was at our house.

Joining the Junior Usher's Board was a major step toward being like Mama. The junior ushers wore navy blue skirts and white blouses. There were certain things that could not be done in the house on Sundays. All preparations for the church had to be done on Saturday. The Sunday dinner was prepared on Saturday evening. Ironing, washing hair, cleaning, and polishing shoes all had to be finished by Saturday evening before bedtime. Everybody had to go to church, starting with Sunday School. Mama realized I had not ironed my skirt or blouse for church one Sunday morning. Having to usher morning and evening in that wrinkled-up skirt and blouse taught me a valuable lesson. Do what your Mama tells you to do or suffer the consequences. Being laughed at through both services that Sunday made me do what Mama said to do for a long time. Teasing lasted a long time after that fateful day. I never forgot to iron my uniform again.

Being on the Junior Usher Board was a job loved and coveted by many. Wearing the uniform, seating churchgoers, and directing the offering was the ultimate. Singing in the choir was the best seat in the house, but ushers had reasons to move around without being scolded. The water cooler was in the back of the church, too, which was another plus. Senior ushers served on Communion Sundays.

The evenings of Communion Sunday seemed to go on forever. Hymn after hymn was raised (sang). During this devotion and serving of the sacrament, it never failed, one of the

Deacons would raise the hymn "There is a Fountain." It was as if the Deacons deliberately mumbled the words to the hymns, always sung in standard meter.

The Deaconesses took turns preparing the sacrament. This was a job for the mother of the church, butsometimes the Mother needed help. In that case, the Deaconess would help in the preparation. Real tiny wine glasses were used, and real bread wafers were eaten at the time of consumption. The last hymn of the night was usually "I Know It Was the Blood."

The next day was Monday, and after breakfast, Mama loaded up a little red wagon with a pot full of peas, rice, and fried chicken. She told us we were going to the Shop. Not knowing what that was, my brother pulled the wagon, and we went to the other end of our street. It was not very far from the house we lived in. Arriving at the Shop, there was a sign at the top. The sign was white written in red letters. It said Division Street Café!

Mama opened the door with a key and took the food into the kitchen. There was a cut-out window from the front of the shop to the kitchen. Mama took orders there at the cut-out and served the food there too. A person eating in the Shop would be served at one of the tables in the front. Customers out front could not see into the back where the kitchen was. The food was put on the stove to stay warm.

Directly in front of and under the cut-out window wasa long metal box. A pan was underneath one end to catch drippings from melting ice. Written on the outside was the word Barq. This was the soda box. Barq was a popular brand of soda pop. The sodas stood tall in the box. There was Coca-Cola, a royal crown (RC), and all the Nehi flavors.

Nehi had grape, orange strawberry, peach, and cream soda!Ice was chipped over the bottles to keep them cool.

There was an electric refrigerator in the shop. The house had an icebox that had to be kept cool by using blocks of ice. The iceman came by every other day with ice on the back of his truck. The ice melted fast in the Florida heat, and water was always dripping from the ice truck. It was puzzling to me for the shop to have an electric refrigerator, and at the house, the water had to be constantly mopped up. It did not matter that a dishpan was under the ice; water still managed to get on the floor. It would be two more years before Daddy was convinced to buy an electric refrigerator for the house!

The big butter cookies at the Shop cost one penny. A butternut candy bar, baby ruth, zero, and a payday all cost a nickel each. A coke (six ounces) was six cents. The bottle was saved and traded back to the delivery man for a penny. All the sodas were in glass bottles. A refund was guaranteed when the man brought more cases of soda. People would scavenge for the bottles the same way people look for aluminum cans these days.

This was the first time my Mama laid down during the day that I can remember. She had to be really tired from all the work she did around the house all the time. The shop sold BC and Stanback headache powders. Mama took a BC and drank a coke each time the trip was made to the shop. Once she took the BC, she would lay down on a little cot by the kitchen door and doze for a little while.

These people had to be rich. Not only did they own a car, a television, and a phone, but a candy store too! Looking at the Mary janes, squirrel nuts, and long boys made our mouths water. Peppermint balls (soft) were two for a penny. There was a slab cookie called "rock and roll." It tastes sort of like ginger bread with hard strawberry icing on top. There were two slabs in each pack. A child could buy a rock and roll and share one slab with a friend or sibling. It cost a nickel, just like the candy bars. The shop also sold cigarettes and cigars. Mama was not happy about this, but Daddy smoked cigars, and he sold them too. He smoked the big fat King Edward brand of cigars. Once Mama woke up; usually, we would be given one of those big butter cookies! It was so good.

The shop was opened almost all day on Saturdays. The special was always pork and beans and rice with a big piece of mullet fish. Hot dogs and hamburgers were sold along with fish sandwiches. Mama's homemade ice cream was loved by everyone and still talked about even now all these years later. It was the best and was made with love.

Each Saturday morning, my brother and I had to turn the handle on the ice cream churn. In a couple of minutes, our arms would be sore. Whoever was lucky that day got to lick what was left after Mama put the ice cream in the freezer. Once in a while, strawberry ice cream was made, but vanilla was made each time. No matter how much was made, it would sell out so fast. If there was any left on a Sunday, it would be sold between Sunday School and church services. The members from all the churches would come to get a cold drink, cookies, chewing gum, or ice cream.

Daddy started work helping build Cape Canaveral (renamed Cape Kennedy after the President was assassinated) shortly after our arrival in Florida. He also kept a lawn service/handyman business on Saturdays. There was no working on Sundays. Daddy maintained the yards of a few rich folks in Winter Park, FL, and would make it home around three on a Saturday.

Daddy had built himself an underground barbeque pit out the back of the shop. During the winter months, not much lawn care was needed, and he would get home much earlier. Some of those times, he would fire up the barbecue pit, and he and his friends would sit around chatting, waiting for the meat to cook. Daddy's barbeque was almost as famous as Mama's ice cream. The moment it was known he was grilling, the orders started coming in. Just like the ice cream, there never seemed to be enough. It was strange to see Daddy preparing food. He never cooked anything at the house. Mama waited on him, "hand and foot," as was said. In my mind, he could not cook, clean up, or wash clothes. The reality was, there were certain things considered to be "woman's work." There were certain things only men, it seemed, were expected to do. Working outside of the house was a man's job. Working anywhere to keep the family comfortable was definitely a job for a woman. Cleaning and cooking were not one of the things a man was expected to do.

The same year of our arrival, Daddy decided to makea cane patch outback of the Shop. He would cut the cane when it was ready, take it to the cane mill in the next town, and make syrup. Sometimes Daddy would take us with him to the cane mill. An old horse pulled the grinding stone around and around. The process was tedious and took all day. Our lunch was one peanut butter "nab" (crackers) and a soda. The dark, beautiful, sweet cane syrup was sold for

$2.50 per gallon. The light color frothy run-off was kept too. It was alcoholic. This drink was called the "mother." Looking back, the cane mill was a cover for an old-fashioned moonshine operation. The syrup was stored in the cool, dry attic of our house.

Selling homemade syrup was another one of the ways Daddy made money. Six gallons of syrup made a profit of $12.50! That much money went a long way back then. Pork neck bones smoked or fresh cost five cents a pound. A loaf of bread was ten cents, and a gallon of gas for the car was twenty-five cents.

There were orange trees in the backyard off from the house. The citrus season would arrive in the autumn. Daddy picked the oranges from his trees each season and sold the fruit. The type of orange and the weight of the fruit determined how much it was worth. Daddy grew a variety called "Possum browns." The fruit was sweet. My brother and me and sometimes Mama would pick the fruit up off the ground. Daddy climbed the ladder with an orange sack positioned across his chest. The oranges would be put in the sack until it was full. The sack would be dumped. The climb down the ladder had to be hard as the sack was full of oranges then. Up and down the ladder picking the fruit took all of one day and half of another day. Some of those trees were very tall. Daddy would go up the ladder and shake the taller trees to make the fruit fall to the ground. The price of the fruit at the juicing plant was determined by whether it was a good or not so good season.

The last car Daddy bought was a 1957 Chevrolet. In the following car-buying years, he bought trucks. A truck allowed for other moneymaking ventures. Owning a truck cut out the fee for ice delivery and hauling fruit to the juice plant. Before buying a truck, another person hauled the fruit for Daddy, and this cut the profit almost in half! The cost of ice delivery was free. The truck was used to help neighbors and friends in our town. It was a time that people helped each other as much as possible.

My first business venture was crocheting scarves to be displayed on coffee and end tables. The entire class of fourth and fifth graders was taught to crochet in Arts and Crafts class.

This was the same class that taught us to play the flutophone. The boys were given the same instructions as the girls. Some of those boys became skilled at crocheting and playing the flutophone. Others just took the failing grade and laughed at the rest of us.

Mama had a huge crocheted, starched scarf on the coffee table in the living room. The end tables had much smaller scarves. Guests wanted to know where Mama had gotten the scarves, and with so much pride, she would let them know. My daughter made this! "Do you think she could make me one?" this lady asked. Mama told her, "yes." Most women carried handkerchiefs during this time. Learning to trim the handkerchiefs in fine crochet thread made more money than the scarves and took less time to complete. The cost was fifty cents for the handkerchiefs and a dollar twenty-five for the medium-sized scarves. It costs $2.50 for a coffee table-sized scarf.

Selling stalks of leftover sugar cane was my second business venture. Daddy told Ben and me to sell the fat ones for a quarter, the medium-sized ones for fifteen cents, and the real skinny ones for a dime. The cane was sold out front of our house. There was a sign made from a piece of a cardboard box. Nobody stood out there to watch for thieves. If someone came along and wanted a stalk, that person would yell to get someone to collect the money. Cutting the cane to sell was not easy. The fine fuzz on the leaves would cut like a razor blade. It was hard not to get cut messing around in the cane patch. Daddy said it was fiberglass. It sure cut deep and would hurt later as it healed.

Once the season was over for harvesting the sugar cane, what was left would be banked for the next season. Banking means laying stalks flat and placing a mound of dirt on top of them, just enough to fully cover the stalks. The new stalks started to grow from the eyes (notches) on the banked stalks in the spring. Sugar cane blowing in the wind is beautiful and sweet to eat. The ones harvesting this crop would suffer from many cuts and bruises. Learning to sew in Home Economics in ninth grade was opening up a new world for me.

Selling sugarcane made a little profit. Payingattention to the Home Economics teacher made a lot moreprofit. The money made from the sugarcane was used to buy cloth, thread, and patterns from the dry goods store. Dry goods stores are comparable to the era's easy in and out stores. Woolworths and Kressege (later shortened to Kress) were the most popular at the time.

There was usually a lunch counter in the store, but people of color could not sit and order or eat there. An order could be placed at the end of the counter, paid for, and taken outside to enjoy. Sit-ins and boycotts took place to protest this treatment. People of color could spend hard-earned "green" money at these places then be forced to eat someplace outside.

Most materials were three yards for a dollar. A lovely dress or skirt and vest might be created from the three yards of material. Mama saw an A-line dress I made in Home Economics and decided that sewing was my talent. A-line and empire-style dresses were in fashion then. The very next thing created by me was a Dashiki of many colors.

It took about thirty minutes to run the seams on a Dashiki. Wearing it to school the next day, everyone wanted to know where it came from. The cost was also debated. The price was $1.75. No one could believe it was a personal creation of mine. This friend was small. The calculation guaranteed two dashikis from each purchase of three yards for a dollar material!

This friend promised if I would make her one, then payment would be made on delivery. And so it was. Making one and sometimes as many as three dashikis each week allowed the creation of styles for myself. Personalizing the Dashikis by adding bric brac was easy.

Mama ordered some clothes from catalogs. Spiegel and Montgomery Ward mail-order catalogs would arrive, and I could look through the magazines with her. The excitement was unmatched. The payment for the order was

C.O.D. (cash on delivery). The order came to the post office. A pink slip would let the customer know the package had arrived. The customer then would go into the post office, pay the required amount and receive the package.

Most of the things ordered were to wear to church or special occasions. An older seamstress lived not far from us. Every year before school started, Mama would take me to get measured for skirts to wear to school. The skirts were all the same, gathered with elastic waists. The only difference was the color or the pattern on the material. By the time of entering ninth grade, my skirts were made by me.

Valuable lessons were taught. Mama and Daddy knew something that had to be learned. Prayer first, then time and consistency are the key ingredients to making a dream come true. There will be down days, but there will also be upbeat days. The times were changing, and so were the attitudes of a new generation of entrepreneurs.

The new generation of forward-thinking individuals was upon us. Fast food hit like a comet from another world.

A sense of urgency guided these new movers and shakers. The desire to hang in and hang on was slipping. Giving up on a dream became the norm for many. Whether it was right or just right now, it guided many dreams into oblivion. Selling dashikis and crocheting kept me up to date in fashion. It also made a little spending money along the way. Falling for a guy would derail a lot of this independence. First, love was puzzling and time-consuming.

A crush, or puppy love, as it was called, became the number one priority. Spending more time thinking about love and the Temptations singing about love was number one. Although good grades continued in high school, the day of completion was the light at the end of the tunnel. Nobody in the family had ever graduated from college. Mama had high expectations that the first college graduate might be me. Attempting to speed up the process of growing up scared Mama.

Mama equated this puppy love with giving up on everything else. Normally girls that got pregnant were mostly kept hidden away at home. Some were able to go to a family that even lived in another town or state. Most times, "good" girls were not allowed to socialize with these prospective new mothers. The girls were ostracized and isolated. Mama did not keep me from being in the company of these friends. There was some curiosity about being with a boy but not enough to consider taking that leap into womanhood. My freedom to roam around was limited already. It was hard to define a difference when a friend found herself "in trouble".

At sixteen, going to a sports event or school-sponsored dance would not happen. The cheering at the gym could be heard at our house. A boy child was allowed to attend games. My brother could go to the games but I could not. Following all the rules got me nowhere. It was not fair at all. A good friend and respected young man decided to help out. The good friend came to the house and asked for permission to take me to the game. Permission was granted.

This friend would pick me up, then go around the corner to his girlfriend. Then the switch would take place with an agreement to meet back there at a certain time. The evening with my boyfriend was good. There was no thought or acting on the notion of making love, at least not by me. The switch-off worked for a few "dates."

The switch offended me when my friend and his girlfriend were late coming back to switch off. Finally arriving home an hour past curfew, the door was locked. Going around to the bedroom window only underscored the lockout with a lot of cussing by daddy. It was very cold sitting on that concrete step from midnight until five a.m. the following day. Mama let me in when she got up. The disappointment covered her like a blanket. Her shoulders curved inward, her walk slow, shaking her head. No words were needed. Never hurting Mama was my intention. I had failed.

Being in love and maturing were such strong influences that it was hard to concentrate on anything else for junior and senior high school years. Several close friends, boys, and girls had advanced to the next step up from puppy love. One or two had gotten pregnant. One or two had gotten girls pregnant. It was clear neither was ready for parenting.

It is ironic that vision is clear when observing situations from a distance. The closer the connection, the cloudier the truth. Mama had a valid reason for concern. The puppy love crush of mine was the son of her best friend. Everyone attended the same church. The same church across the street from home. The most compelling negative was the age difference. There was six years of separation in age. Most would assume it was a young girl being taken advantage of. Neither set of parents could understand that no real action had been taken in this affair.

The parent's concern was validated years later when it was revealed that each husband in these marriages was considerably older than the wife. There was fourteen years difference for my parents and a few years difference for my future husband's parents. This was comparable to a man chasing a child. It was up to the girl to stop the infatuation no matter who was chasing after the other. It was as if the man's parents were against the partnering as much as my parents were.

Mama felt that if this were allowed to continue, her daughter would get married, have children and never go to college. Two friends got married when the woman realized a baby was on the way. My boyfriend and me were the witnesses on their marriage certificate. A hidden relationship continued for us, and marriage was always a part of this conversation.

By this time, Mama had stopped running the shop. Mama took a job at the hospital in foodservice. The shop was leased to another family as a restaurant and sweet shop with an expanded menu. Leaving school one day, hanging out with friends got me home in just the dark. The kitchen was cleaned, all the food was put away. Mama said, "Don't touch anything in that kitchen since you think you are grown; you should eat where you have been." Going to bed hungry, I cried until sleep took over me.

I came home much earlier the next day but still later than the expected time. Bringing home cheeseburgers from the Shop was a mistake. I thought there would be no food for me as the day before. Mama was convinced that I had taken money from a man to buy the food! All of my protests fell on deaf ears. Then Mama said living there and taking money from some man would not be accepted. She cried. I cried. Hearing the hurt in her made me decide to move out.

My first set of luggage was two Winn Dixie brown bags. I did not want to continue to hurt my Mama. She had been too good to me. I moved out the next day. I moved into a bedroom with no running water, no indoor toilet and no real privacy. I was a junior in high school justa few days from summer break. I got a job cleaning a houseonce a week on Friday.

The pay was eleven dollars. I did not go to school on Fridays. The rent was three dollars per week. Paying the rent and my ride to the job left me six dollars. I bought a few things to eat and always bought one yard of material to make me an outfit. Independence was very important. Cleaning that house kept me independent until the floor was expected to be mopped on hands and knees. Refusal to do this was met with frowns and huffing. I quit!

During this same time, the friends who had gotten married were blessed with a beautiful little boy. The pressure to get married was amped up. Just finishing the eleventh grade, moving out, and turning sixteen was enough for me. The new mother talked about going to Adult Education classes in the fall. It sounded really great. Course work will be completed that upcoming January. This meant the certificates of completion would be issued five months before the graduating class at the High School.

Two of my older sisters lived in New York City. New York sounded so glamorous and exciting. A trip to visit was at the top of the list. The plan was to go when the weather was warm. It was decided that June or July was perfect.

Looking forward to that trip is an understatement. There was no baby in the making and, in fact, no sexual consummation. It was settled that July was the month to visit New York.

During this period, Mama came to convince me to move back home. The big move was one mile from home.

Everyone in town knew what had happened. Mama stressed the fact that moving back home was always possible with the blessings of her and daddy. Moving out of the house did not remove the love, and caring mama had for me. Plans to go to New York were already in place. The move back home did not happen until much later, after the marriage and the miscarriage.

My fiancé revealed a fear that if the New York trip happened, a return was not guaranteed. Wanting to start a better life there was a part of the plan. It was met with so much resistance from my partner. Finally, an ultimatum was given. Marriage had to happen before the ticket would be bought. An agreement was reached. Marriage and a two-week trip to New York was the deal.

Marriage at the Orange County Courthouse was at 1 p.m. on Friday, July 18, 1969. High school class rings were exchanged as wedding rings. Being allowed to come into the Kress Store cafeteria now, a giant banana split was shared. This was the only special thing done on that day. The bus ticket was purchased at departure and cost thirty-one dollars from Orlando to New York City. This marriage was consummated only twelve hours after getting married an adventure to the big city was started. The bus left the station at 1 a.m. that Saturday morning. Excitement overruled the fear of traveling to unknown places.

The bus trip took twenty-three hours. The bus stopped at places that did not even have a station building, just a sign with a greyhound on it. Passengers of color would come out of the woods once the bus stopped. Fear was on the faces of these riders. Paying and taking a seat on the bus, one could almost hear a collective release of breath. Sharing the bathroom with all the others on the bus was the only negative throughout the entire trip. Arrival at Grand Central Station at 1 a.m. with a trunk was catastrophic.

The trunk was unloaded and placed there for me. It was very heavy. Lots and lots of people were hurrying every which way. A few glanced at the lady with the trunk and kept walking fast. Larry (my brother-in-law) was supposed to be there with a picture of me. Having never met Larry, I did not know what he looked like. I called Bertha, my sister, and asked what Larry was wearing.

Bertha said that her husband was wearing khaki pants and a yellow shirt with a picture of me in his hand. The first person is seen with this get-up on, minus the picture was a white guy. I asked, "Excuse me, are you, Larry?" He just looked at me and hurried to wherever he

was going. I figured sitting still was the best option and so sat on the trunk and waited. A tall, big man came barreling around the corner.

The big man had something in his hand and looked down at it periodically. The man had on khaki pants and wore a yellow shirt. Both of us started talking at once! My sister's husband had found me. He had to weigh at least

350lbs. and stood 6ft. 4in. He grabbed the trunk and put it on his shoulder. He informed me that a train would take us about a block from the apartment. The trunk was heavy, but he never complained.

Arriving at the apartment at two-thirty in the morning, my brother-in-law tried to get a few hours of sleep. He had to be on the train to Manhattan by seven a.m. My sister and I had not seen each other in ten years. The last time was when they lived in Charleston, and I was seven and she was 28 years old. The resemblance was once unmistakable. Another sister, Cora, lived in Brooklyn too. There was alsoa brother John that lived on Long Island.

A two-week trip to New York turned into sevenweeks of hoping my husband would come to join me there.He refused. Fear of something new would not allow a dream to unfold. Each call home was the same. There was always the uncertainty of my return. Near the end of August, the temperature at night started to cool down. The pleas that I return home to Florida increased.

The first time the ultimatum was given for me to come home to Florida, the money was wired to me byWestern Union. I got the money and held on to it for abouta week. My partner had sent fifty dollars. Going grocery shopping with my sister Bertha one day, I spent some of themoney. There were things I wanted in the store and so I bought them. A week later, half of the bus ticket money hadbeen spent. Still, my husband refused to even consider the idea of coming to New York.

All of the time spent in New York was amazing. Learning how to go places by bus and on the subway alone was my ultimate. This was my first time riding the train. The train moved so fast. Navigating between my two sister's apartments made me feel just like a real city girl. All of the family would be nervous and try to convince me not to travel alone in the city. The opportunity only presented itself once or twice. It was exhilarating.

Pressure started immediately to convince me to come home. Finally, an agreement was made. The agreement was, my husband would find us our own place there in

Florida, and I would come home. I was not going back to that room rented when I was in the eleventh and twelfth grade. A week later, my husband assured me he had found us a place, so I went home.

The place was in a rooming house in the next town. It smelled old and musty. Everyone on the second floor shared the kitchen and bathroom. Listening to the radio and reading all day while he worked became so boring. By the time my husband arrived home, I wanted to go someplace, any place! Usually, he was tired and did not want to go anywhere. At nineteen years of age, being couped up in a room all day was no fun at all.

Getting out of the rooming house for a few hours was alright with me. Just going to my mother-in-law's house was not the solution. My husband would do whatever his Mom asked him to do. Fix something in the house or do something in the yard. He would then sit in a chair and sleep or pretend to be asleep. Sometime later, he would decide it was time to leave and go back to the rooming house.

Living in the rooming house had to come to an end. I hated it there. Feeling sick on the stomach one day all day, I imagined the smells and the building was making me sick.

Moving out of the place a couple of weeks later made me smile. It was about the same time I realized I might be pregnant. It was confirmed by the doctor the next week. There was always an unsettled feeling inside my stomach. Ginger ale, saltines, and nothing else worked to settle my belly. It is hard to explain the feeling, but just the idea of food was enough to cause a trip to the bathroom.

At this time, the realization and proof that my partner was cheating were revealed quite an by accident. Knowing something was wrong in the way I was being treated, it never occurred that this man was cheating. He begged to get married, always talked about wantingchildren, and I was pregnant. My inexperience in life and relationships made it impossible to recognize the signs of infidelity. Normally my days would be spent at my mother-in-law's house. It was agreed that spending time alone and feeling so bad all the time was not a good idea. I was dropped off each morning to spend the day while he worked.

A lot of time was spent lying down, just trying not to feel so sick. My husband had agreed to put up a storage shed in the backyard of his sister-in-law's house. Normally I would just stay and wait for him to return to pick me up.

He asked if I wanted to go, so sure, I would not want to go.I said yes. That seemed to upset him, and he came up withall kinds of negative reasons why I might not want to go. One reason was that there would not be any place to lie down. I said I would lie down in the car if I had to.Realizing my mind was made up, he sped up the street reallyfast.

Our arrival was the same. Speeding up to the house,he jumped out of the car. He had not said a word to me the entire thirty-minute drive but glanced at me every now and then with pure hate. This shocked me. My husband had been a moody person all the time of our knowing each other. This was different somehow.

I went inside to use the bathroom a while after we arrived for him to put the shed up. Coming out of the bathroom, the phone rang. The young lady, our niece, picked it up and said "hello," listened for a minute, then said, "hold on." The phone was handed to me, and my niece said, "this call is for Uncle James (my husband)." Putting the receiver to my ear, I said, "hello." The woman on the other end said, "I want to talk to James." I explained that I was his wife and that she could tell me what it was she wanted. I thought it was a side job prospect. The woman screamed at me and said again that she wanted to talk to James. I asked her who she was and she told me she was his girlfriend. I told her she was not going to talk to him and anything she had to say to him, she could say it to me. I hung the phone up then.

• • •

The hurt and embarrassment of it all were just too much. I started to throw up right then and thereafter fighting not to all morning. Going outside, I told my husband that his girlfriend had just called and told her not to call there anymore. He told me I did not have the right to do that! The hate turned to a burning red in his eyes. He threw the tool he had in his hand on the ground and jumped in the car. We were on the far side of town. It looked like he was trying to leave me there. I went around the car and got in.

Our niece stood in the doorway, saw all of this, and just stood there puzzled. James yelled out of the window to say that he would finish the job the next day. He sped off, driving recklessly, shifting gears and swinging around corners, jerking me from side to side in the car. No words were spoken until the ride was almost over. I told him that he should have been honest with me while I was in New York and from the very beginning. He reached over me, opened the car door, and tried to shove me out! The car was weaving all across the road. I was scared then. The shock of it all had me fighting not to throw up in the car. He picked up my scissors off of the car seat and held them in a stabbing way. He held it with his hands clenched around the handle staring at me. I prayed to make it to his Mama's house and did not speak again until we got there. Once again, he jumped out of the car. I could hear his Mama ask where I was. I was too sick to move just yet. I was drained and weak from the hurt and shock of it all.

His Mama knew something awful had happened that day. I could never tell her exactly what had happened. Being four months pregnant did not make the sick feeling subside. In fact, it seemed to get worse. The doctor could not explain it. He did reveal that there were fibroid tumors growing inside at the same rate as my baby. I knew nothing about tumors.

Learning about fibroid tumors was important to me.I wanted my baby to grow faster, grow stronger and outgrow the tumors. The doctor said if the tumors grew faster than my baby, the tumors would strangle the baby, and I would spontaneously abort. A forced miscarriage is what the doctor called it. All of this scared me tremendously.

The doctor said that if this miscarriage happened, it might be for the best. He said there was no way to know what effect these tumors had on my baby. I cried and cried. How could losing my baby be for the best? All of this stress worrying about this and that did not help. The doctor had me coming in every week to check my baby and me. I miscarried my only male child at five and a half months. Having spent the night at my mother in law's house, the nauseous feeling was overwhelming. The cramps were even worse.

Late morning was more of the same sick feelings. Stepping into the bathroom my stomach clenched while trying to make it to the toilet. Once I made it, a large amount of liquid plopped into the bowl. When I looked down, the toilet bowl was filled with very dark blood. It was scary. My mother-in-law came to see what had me so scared. She concluded that me and the baby were in trouble. Laying in bed with my legs propped up is how my husband found me when he got off work. His Mama told him to take me to the doctor. The angry look was back.

Having been placed on the back seat of the car, wrapped in a sheet, it seemed the cramps had eased considerably. My mother-in-law periodically cautioned her son to slow down. Muttering something, he kept speeding. A few minutes later, he slammed on the brakes, throwing me off the seat and onto the floor. His Mama screamed for him to stop the car, but I knew there was no use. My baby was outside of me now. Entering the emergency room, there was a lot of blood on the sheet that was wrapped around me. My mother- in law went in and grabbed a wheelchair, helped me get in it, and pushed me into the emergency room. She loved me and took care of me as if I were her own child. My husband stood there looking blank-faced.

My mother-in-law told my Mama what had happened. My Mama told me to come home and let her take care of me. I went home to my Mama and daddy. Daddy was actually compassionate during this time, always asking how I was feeling. Throughout the time knowing him, he had never shown much emotion toward me. The two of them had lost babies over the years, so perhaps he understood this feeling of loss. Living in my old room was nice. Staying there until time to go to Duke Research Center was therapeutic.

At my checkup, the doctor determined that there were still some problems. A dilation and curettage were done, but the fibroids kept growing and spreading. I still felt pregnant, just not nauseous. There were some trial studies being conducted at Duke University. The focus was on helping women with issues that were similar to mine. The diagnosis was fibroid tumors that had developed into cervical cancer. I was nineteen years old.

The doctor advised me to try the Duke trials; otherwise, there was nothing else to do. Before leaving for Duke and after the research study there, I was advised that becoming pregnant again might never happen. Explaining this to my Mama and his Mama was hard. My Mama wanted to go with me to Duke. I refused. My Mama gave me some money and told me to let her know whenever I needed anything. I did not want my Mama to be there in case I got worse. My husband was allowed to come to Duke, but I could tell he did not really want to go. There was no guarantee that I would return home at all. Everybody was scared. These were clinical trials with experimental medicines using myself and others as guinea pigs. If this experimentation would give me a chance to become a mother, then I would be willing to try it.

Circumstances were a lot different on this bus trip to Duke University. There was none of that excitement from the New York trip. Durham, NC, is a long way from

Oviedo, FL. The stay in the hospital for women's studies was from three to six weeks, depending on how the body reacted to the medicines. A transport picked two other ladies and me up from the Greyhound bus station. One lady was from Georgia. The other was from somewhere in North Carolina.

It was a beautiful sunny summer day when the transporter dropped us off at the admissions office. During the admission and room assignment process, I only saw two other black people. Neither was anywhere near as dark as me, and both had beautiful long hair. I was the only occupant in the room for one full day. The medicines were started that same evening. The next day a roommate was assigned to the room. The roommate was maybe five feet tall and eighty-five pounds soaking wet. Her personality was big enough to make up the difference, though.

My roommate introduced herself as Mrs. Betty Simms. She was there to have all her female parts removed, she told me. The complete hysterectomy was scheduled for the next morning. She said she was tired of the parts causing problems and so much pain. There was no plan for more children. The roommate and her husband already had three children. Listening and laughing with her caused the anxiety in me to ease. My God puts the right people in place at just the right time for us. Betty was so full of energy and funny stories about her husband and children.

A few hours before meeting this woman, I was crying in my pillow balled up in my bed. Now here I was laughing as though an old friend had surprised me with a visit. The roommate's surgery was scheduled for the next day. She decided that her husband should bring us seafood platters for dinner. I explained that I did not have much money and did not want to order anything. Betty explained that her husband was paying for dinner and would bring it at seven o'clock after he got off from work.

Shortly after seven o'clock, a tap on the door let us know someone was visiting. None of my family was in Durham, so this had to be someone coming to visit my roommate. A tall man entered the room carrying a large brown bag and an overnight case. The man was my roommate's husband. The man greeted me and went to his wife. Betty introduced us and brought my food to my bedside. Betty just bubbled with enthusiasm. She informed her husband that once I was released from the hospital, the two of them were having me over for dinner. His name was Tommy, and it was alright with him to have a stranger over for dinner. I suppose whomever Betty cared for, he cared for.

Betty went home after three days. She would call to check on me periodically. Betty warned me not to try leaving Durham without coming to her house for dinner. Their house was on a main street in the downtown area. The greyhound bus station was just around the corner from their house. A set of steps lead up to the door from the street. After my release from the research center, I went straight to my newfound friend's house. Dinner was delicious, and the children treated me as if they had known me a long time. It felt like being with family. The bus to home was leaving at 9 p.m. As the time drew closer, I gathered my things, and Tom walked me the half block to the bus station. He waited with me until I was safely on the bus.

The research trial lasted twenty-one days. Before release from the hospital, the doctors explained that time would tell if the medicine worked. The tender soreness in my mouth had stopped. I was able to eat and drink something other than water, milk, grits, and unsalted crackers. I was looking forward to eating something other than hospital food.

I met Betty and Tom's children. The same spirit that flowed through the parents flowed through them. The children acted like I was just one of their parent's many friends. It did not seem to matter that it was their first time meeting me. Betty cooked baked ham, candied yams, collard greens, macaroni and cheese, potato salad, cornbread, and rice. A friend had also baked a beautiful cake. Music was playing quietly in the background. This felt like home already. The bus to Florida was leaving in a couple of hours, but I did not want to miss it. I hurried to eat and socialize with the few family members there.

Betty packed me lunch for the long bus trip and some sodas wrapped in foil. My appreciation of her and the consideration of her entire family remains a sweet spot in my life. Tom walked me around the corner to the bus depot, asked if I would be okay, and wished me well. Sadly after a few letters exchanged between us, contact was lost. It cannot be proven but, looking back, I believe my husband destroyed letters from Betty. His need to control me would override everything. When I had told him about the people that treated me so kindly, it was as if he got a negative attitude about the whole encounter that was a true blessing to me. It was as though he was jealous that someone had been there to make a very difficult journey easier. Upon my return, my excitement ofhaving met these lovely people was dampened by his uninterest.

The only other personal connection made at Duke was a friendship with a beautiful nursing school student. The student was working there at the Women's Research Hospital. She was only nineteen years old, just like me. This nurse knew that most of the women at the hospital were there for surgery or treatment for cancer. Telling her my story, I could see that she was scared for me in her eyes. Cancer was a death sentence for many during these times. No matter what form of cancer was attacking the body, research was just not advanced enough to save many patients.

My Lord and Savior kept me through it all. He saved me from this thing that ravages the body. There were moments of unexplained sadness that lasted way more than a moment. Keeping all this depression hidden from everyone was getting harder. Not wanting to worry Mama,

I acted like everything was alright. I did not know then what I know now.

What I know is that I had been granted favor, mercy, grace, and undeserved love and kindness from my God! A short while after returning home, the doctor let me know the medicine was successful. The cancerous cells had been killed. There were no more tumors but a guarantee of motherhood was unlikely. This was not the news I wanted to hear. The Lord had kept me here for a reason. I did not reach the age of twenty until six months later. I suppose the selfishness of youth made the wish for more a reasonable thought!

Sitting at home as a lot of women chose to was not my thing. Reading everything in sight, including the Bible,kept me busy for a time. It was as if the rest of the world had kept moving forward, and moving along was expected of me. Meanwhile, folks around me wanted to know what my plan was. The truth is, there was no plan. How dare they think there was some reason to be more than a wife and hopefully a mother. It did not occur to me that I could do these and so much more. My thinking had been constricted to the box I lived in. My brain may as well have been chained up only to escape through reading books.

There is a lot of magic in reading. One may be transported to worlds created by the power of reading. It is almost like going fishing with the mind. In my opinion, casting out a line to reel in a fish happens to be one of the most soothing pleasures. Opening a book casts the mind and reels in the universe. Living everywhere made it bearable to live anywhere. Reading had filled and soothed my heart even as a young girl, unable to go many places. Two months after my return from Duke, I got a job at the new university near our town.

Starting at the University was an outlet. Mama could not hold back the enthusiasm. Realizing that my starting there was actually working in the cafeteria, the excitement turned to disappointment. The realization set in that I was not a student, just an employee. Mama had probably told her friends that her daughter was going to University. I suppose it appeared that a lie had been told. However, the pride returned as promotions were fast-paced.

Preparing breakfast and lunch for the University students and administrators made independence possible. My money was, after all, my money. This was a time when sewing was still very much a part of my existence. Going into a fabric shop to buy whatever suited me fueled the creative juices. Still, I felt my Mama needed to see me doing more.

Mama saw something in me that I did not see yet. This desire to do more and be more still rested somewheredeep inside. Glimpses of this person would show themselves sporadically as help was given to someone in the community. The help could be as simple as writing a letter for a person who could not write. It could be as basic as taking an old lady to the grocery store. It was the real me emulating my Mama who helped when she could.

Knowing that reaching the level of Mama's giving heart was not possible, just trying to be like her was enough. It was enough for that time, at least. My husband would always question the good deeds and smear them. The smear would happen when he wanted to know how much the person had paid me. Often, I would lie about an amount of payment just not to hear some lecture. Most times, I would just say I was not paid anything. He would go on and on about the price of gas. The time spent could have been spent at our house doing something there. A constant reminder of the size of our small house would shut him up. There was only one bedroom, a living room, kitchen, and bathroom. The house and yard were kept clean and presentable. Ambition would rear its head time and time again as I fought to be a good wife.

A lack of ambition in my husband was the main reason Mama and Daddy were against our being together. It was becoming clear to me that they were right. What theydid not know was that control was an issue as well. There was no true partnership. Making money on my own was never seen as a positive thing. It was perceived as a threat. A one-sided partnership is doomed to failure. It is especially doomed when one of the partners is stillmaturing.

A decision I made to start college began the downfall of this marriage. My partner knew once again what I did not know. He knew that putting myself in the real world interacting with others was moving us farther apart. His refusal to be a part of this growth was unacceptable.

❖ ❖ ❖

Talking about it did not help. His solution was to let us just not do this. Never willing to explore new ideas, he would sit at home sulking. The love of learning something new kept my spirits up. Married life was turning into a downer. Either I had to fit into some preconceived mold or pretend to be happy.

A time came when it did not seem worth all this effort of pretending. Whatever worked for those around us was certainly not working for us. Conversations were minimal. Always a big girl, by this time, morbid obesity had reared its head. The satisfaction felt from food was better than the relationship itself.

Starting college was the best thing for me. Paying for my classes myself without the use of any student loans was a big deal. The car was shared by my husband and me. Some of my classes, in the beginning, were evening classes. Classes started at 7:00 p.m. My partner got off work at 4:00 p.m. every day. On more than one occasion, he would get home with the car just a few minutes before class was scheduled to start. The college was a thirty-minute drive from our house! It was a deliberate attempt to sabotage my efforts to get a degree.

The third semester my tuition money was lost because of absences. It hurt a lot because it was so mean. The economics professor did give me some good advice. He advised that withdrawing from classes was better than receiving a failing grade. This professor would lecture in the monotone of a robot. He let me know that he was a real human being, though. My appreciation for this kind man was greatly appreciated many years later.

Even though my partner and I still lived in the house together and shared the same bed, the space between us was widening. Rarely did we attend church together. Our church was right across the street from the house. By now, I was twenty- two years old, cancer-free, and still not pregnant. Talking to Mama about school one day had me crying my eyes out. Mama was afraid for me. I assured her everything was alright, but I had lost my tuition money.

When I told her why I had lost my tuition money, she just shook her head. She advised me to buy my own car with my own money. Knowing that I worked, she wanted to know how much money I had in the bank. I guessed maybe twenty dollars. I worked five days a week. Realizing my response was hesitant and senseless, Mama told me to open my own separate bank account as she and Daddy had all these years. Mama was shocked at the fact that I did not have but a few dollars. Mama gave me some money that day. I had already lost my tuition, but my intentions were to return to school the next semester. I bought a car for 80.00 dollars. The man wanted $120.00, but all I had was $80.00.

He accepted that I would pay the rest in a week with the agreement.

I drove my 1953 Chevy Bel Air into the yard on the day. It was dirty and rusty but ran like a well-oiled sewing machine. My partner wanted to know how the car was paid for. I explained that I paid for it with my money. The derogatory talk about the way the car looked did not phase me. It was mine, and I never had to be late for school again. I enrolled for the next semester at college. A close friend of ours was attending the same college. He needed a ride one evening as his car would not start. The next time another friend needed a ride to evening classes, my partner had this problem. This guy was the same guy that helped us see each other when I was still in high school. He was the other half of the switch! I finished the semester but did not register for the upcoming semester.

I took my very next paycheck and did what Mama said. I opened a bank account in my name only. Three weeks later, I bought a brand-new car and drove it off the showroom floor. Working at the new development of Disney World paid top dollar. The divide between my partner and me was getting wider.

Still coexisting, the lives of two people could not have been further apart. Putting in many hours at Disney kept me quite busy. My role as a wife was shrinking. Working sometimes twelve and often times fourteen hours per day was exhausting. A day off meant cleaning the house, doing laundry, and sleeping. There was still time for partying at twenty-three years old. There was money in my bank account and my pocket. Life was good.

There are times in life when a person needs to slow down. Sometimes it is not possible to do this on your own. In some instances, the Lord will slow you down. Just pray He does not slow you to a dead halt. Working all those days

* * *

back-to-back and sleeping a few hours, like a twenty-three-year-old, my body was tired. My marriage was pretty much over. My partner was finally convinced to move out and leave me alone. I headed home one night overtired and anticipating two days off from work.

Three months would go by before I would ever see home again. A terrible car accident kept me in the hospital a long time. It seems going asleep behind the wheel, the car ended up in some trees with me wedged into the driver's seat unconscious. A Florida State Trooper found me there at five o'clock, which hurt very badly. Later I would remember the last time I was clear and awake; it was 1:30 a.m. I was in the car alone. I remembered looking at this woman hurt so badly, bloodied, and no one was coming to help her. Watching this hurt woman watching me, I heard a voice say, "Ms. Rouse, can you hear me?" I think I nodded my head. I am not sure about this. The voice said, "I am Officer Randall with the Florida Highway Patrol and help is on the way."

I woke up in the hospital several hours later. There was a big mirror mounted on the wall. I could see someone all bandaged up with only the eyes showing through. My Mama was at the foot of the bed crying along with some others. I told her not to cry that I was going to be alright. She cried more and began to thank God out loud. I suppose I lost consciousness again. The next time I was awake, Mama and my husband were there and a lot of doctors around the bed.

* * *

The doctors explained that more surgery was needed, and it would have to be done with as little anesthesia as possible. Apparently, the first surgery had taken almost six hours, and it was too dangerous to put me under again. My size would require more anesthesia than was safe. At this same time, it was explained that these doctors would try to save my leg but chances were slim that I would ever walk again. Another specialist separated from the group and told me that my pelvis was in so many little pieces that there was no way I could ever have a baby. This made me cry. The group of six doctors left the room with one patting me gently on the shoulder.

Whenever no one was in the room with me, I would cry about the fact that I would not have children. I had already dismissed the fact that walking might not be possible if my leg could be saved. There was only pain for a long time. Physical pain was off the charts, and heart-hurting pain was worse. One day it dawned on me that these doctors do not know everything! I was going to walk, and I was going to have children! It did not matter that I had been told four years earlier at Duke Hospital that I might not be able to have children. After the initial shock wore off, it did not occur to me that the doctors knew what they were talking about. Talk about a hard head; mine was the hardest.

This surgery without anesthesia was a guaranteed screamer. The pain of having three twelve-inch rods screwed into the thigh bone is indescribable. There was no anesthesia except a topical numbing gel that numbed the first two to three inches. The bone could not be numbed. It hurt a lot. Tears started to fall immediately. The vibration of the drill was strange, but there was not a lot of blood pouring out. There was a constant slow stream coming down. The second rod was positioned to go in. Gritting my teeth did not lessen the pain. I must have passed out at some point because I awoke to doctors everywhere.

The doctors were attaching weights to the rods to align the bone as it knitted back together. A section of thigh bone had been broken. There were also rods at the end of the foot of the same leg. A steel rod was placed through the bone below the knee of the same leg. Adjustments could be made as needed by adding weights or taking away weights. X-rays of the bone had to be taken regularly. There was so much equipment on, and in my bed, it was decided that I had to have my own room. Technicians would bring the x-ray machine to my room to take the pictures. There was a large room for patients in traction, but my equipment took up too much space.

The relief from the pain only came while sleeping. Each waking moment was filled with excruciating pain. Thanking God for even being alive to feel the pain was an all-day practice. The morphine acted as a sleeping aid. It did little to stop the pain, but the sleep was therapeutic. Sleep and pray. There was not much crying then. The doctors told me the hospital stay might be six weeks.

Five weeks had passed with me in traction twenty-four hours a day laying on my back. The doctors told me that the bones were healing very well. When asked if I would be going home in a week, the doctors looked at each other. The news given to me was that it was taking longer than was first estimated. Now it was believed the bone needed eight to ten weeks to heal. This news made me cry. I was more than ready to go home. I decided to shop for a new car.

The insurance company underestimated how long hospitalization could last. The first check from the company came directly to me at my home address. Asking my husband to bring a new car book to the hospital, I began shopping for a new car. My Mama and the rest of my circle were horrified. The fact that I was even contemplating getting behind the wheel again shocked them all. The wreck was that bad. My broken body was evidence of this.

The wreck was so bad that it made front-page news in our local newspaper. The word had gotten around that I was looking to buy a new car. Some friends and family decided that I needed to see just how bad the wreck had been. Someone brought the news article to the hospital. Now I was shocked at the condition of the car and the condition of my broken body. I kept looking for a small, not too expensive car anyway. Mama just looked worried. She had never really driven a car and did not understand why I wanted to keep driving. A Ford Pinto hatchback was purchased some days later. My husband was able to position the car near the hospital room window so that I could see it. It was sporty and small but not too small.

Being in the hospital stuck in bed in traction, the weight started to just melt away. Friends were asked not to bring unhealthy foods to the room. The friends complied. They would bring fruit, sugar-free candy, money, and a joint (weed) every now and then. Of course, I had to send the joints home for safekeeping until I got out of the hospital. Although being in the hospital for a long time, there was never one day when loneliness made me sad. There were visitors at all times of day and night.

The hospital staff just stopped trying to control the comings and goings of my huge circle of friends, family, and associates. The walls in the room were covered with get-well cards. So many floral arrangements came that some would be shared with other patients. My husband had wound his way back into a partnership with me. All the days I was there would find him there too after work. This was above and beyond what one might expect, especially being separated at the time of the wreck. The hospital staff let him stay as much as he wanted. Meals were ordered for him on a regular basis if he was in the room. He was never charged for any of this.

Eight weeks in traction came and passed. I was still in the bed on my back and still in traction. I had managed to lose sixty pounds. Mama worked there at the hospital, so she came in to see me every day that she worked. She did not look so worried anymore.

One Saturday afternoon, as I was taking a nap, someone cleared their throat. The nurse peeked around this very tall man and asked if it was okay for him to talk to me. I agreed not knowing who this tall white man was. I did not recognize the woman with him either. He said, "Mrs. Rouse my name is Officer Randall with the Florida Highway Patrol." "I am the one who found you that morning, and I never imagined that you had survived that awful wreck." He introduced the lady as his wife. He told me that no one had called in a wreck that morning. He was just driving on his regular rounds and saw my car smashed into the trees. He stopped to see if anyone was alive and found me moaning in pain. His wife started talking then. Mrs. Randall told me that since Officer Randall had found me that morning, he was disturbed by how hurt I was when he found me. Apparently, the condition he found me in stayed in his mind. He thought I had died from my injuries. A friend of his wife worked at the hospital and mentioned the miraculous recovery of a car accident victim. Finding out more about this person and the name, the officer knew it was me. The couple visited for a while. They said a prayer with me, and I was able to thank him for finding me that morning. I had been there hurt badly for hours before he found me.

A chill comes over my body, remembering the way consciousness would come and go during that time before Officer Randall found me. It was as though someone was watching all that time. I was not alone out there after all.

God had kept me while I waited. He had kept me lucid enough to know of His mighty presence. Thank you, Lord.

Ten weeks in traction. The doctors think maybe twelve weeks should be sufficient for the bones to align.

The leg was saved. It was still uncertain if it would accommodate the weight of walking. There were no guarantees, even now. Plans were made to go shopping for new clothes. The weight loss meant that nothing was going to fit anymore.

Getting to the store was not a problem. Although I could not walk yet, I was determined to get there. The doctors did not extend the time. Twelve weeks was the time to take the weights off and the rods out of my thigh. The day had arrived. The weights were removed from every position. The rods were drilled out as they had been drilled in. It hurt so much worse coming out than going in. The next morning was tilt board time.

The tilt board was designed to get the blood flowing to the head again. A subtle adjustment in angling was started. I was scared when I was placed on a tilt board and wheeled to physical therapy to start the process. Lying about feeling dizzy got me right back in the room in about thirty minutes. The legs were weak, and I was about to pass out. The body was strapped to the board, so there was no chance of hitting the floor.

The injuries and laying in the prone position for so many months had further weakened the core of the body.

The faint feeling would come again and again as attempts were made to get the body upright. Using a walker and a strap at the waist, a trip to the bathroom was a success. How proud I was to be able to accomplish this that is takenfor granted by many. Taking a shower later that day was the first full cleaning in three months. Don't get me wrong,the care received from the nurses was top notched. This bears mention here because this time was the few years following the passage of the Civil Rights Act. Some becamemore creative at the ill-treatment of people of color. Living in the deep south, one would expect at least one bad incidentin three months at the hospital, but it did not happen to me.

Physical therapists taught me to walk using my upper body strength to move me along. During the three months in traction, emphasis was placed on strengthening the upper body. This served me well now. A few days later, I could get in and out of bed unassisted but monitored. The orthopedist assured me that I could go home in just one more week! I was so happy!

The day had finally come. I was going home. It was Halloween Day 1973. So anxious to get out of the hospital, the pressure was increased on my husband to pick me up early the next morning. The doctor warned that any fall would require a trip to the emergency room. The doctor sent me home with a walker, wheelchair, and a walking cane. The bones were still very delicately healing. A fall of any kind justified an x-ray. Other than that, an appointment to see the orthopedist was scheduled for three weeks. The back steps at the house had only two steps. These two steps were approximately eighteen inches wide.

My husband picked up our nephews. Both were strong teenagers. He figured the three of them would just carry me into the house. My insistence that I could walk up the two steps convinced him to let me try it. I got up the steps using the walker and then careened off the top step onto the ground! No one was more shocked than me. Lucky for me, the therapists had taught me how to fall. Realizing that I was going to hit the ground, my body was angled away from the badly damaged left side. My husband was trying to convince my nephews to help him get me back in the car for a trip to the emergency room. Laying on my good side, I asked my nephew to bring a chair out of the kitchen. As soon as the chair was brought and placed near, I struggled and with help was able to get in it.

Everybody was in a panic. They were trying to figure how to get me to the car to return to the hospital. Well, I was not going back there. I had only been out of there two hours, and it did not feel like anything new was broken. Sitting there for a while, my Daddy came home, saw me sitting outside, and asked if I was okay. The blabber mouth, my husband, told him I had just fallen off the top step. Daddy was told what the doctor had said about falling.

Trying to hide the fact that the pain was bad, I sat there laughing and happy to be home. The pain pills were there. If I complained, my husband would try to take me back to the hospital. Daddy was naturally concerned but convincing him I was alright; he tried to figure a way to get me in the house. He came up with the idea of building a makeshift ramp out of two by eight boards leftover from remodeling. My nephews brought the wheelchair from the car. The two of them then told my husband they would just carry me into the house in the wheelchair. So they lifted me up, wheelchair and all, and put me in the kitchen. One nephew was fifteen, and the other was seventeen.

Waiting until I could sneak and take a pain pill, the chance presented itself. It hurt so bad by then, and I took two. A few minutes later, I sat on the side of the bed. Finally, lay down in the bed, exhausted but not hurting as bad anymore. My husband decided to drink a beer; later, I drank two beers. Much later, I had a shot of Bacardi rum too. That night our oldest daughter was conceived.

Two days later, my nephews came over to see me. I had them help me to the new car I had bought. Driving us to the mall by the time of arrival, I was feeling unsettled inside. The boys got me in the wheelchair and took me into the Lane Bryant store. Picking out several pants and shirts, a trip to the fitting room was next. The clerk asked if I needed help in the fitting room. I told her no that I could manage. Later my nephew was leaning over me, asking if I was alright. There was no memory of losing consciousness.

The clerk had seen my nephew bring me into the store and go sit outside the store. When I passed out, she found him there. By this time, I was awake. He tried to get me to allow the people to call an ambulance, but I said no. My nephew did not have a license, but he could drive. I toldhim to drive us back home, and he did. It was approximately ten miles from home. The sick feeling was still there. We made it home safe. His driving made me even more nauseous. Hiding the clothes bought at the mall, I lay down. My nephew stayed there until almost time for my husband to come home from work. Since I still could not walk unassisted, it was normal to find me lying in bed.

My husband did not know I had gone to the mall until the week of the doctor's appointment.

The appointment with the orthopedist was two days away. The closer to the office we got the more charged the atmosphere was. The receptionist checked us in and left us in the waiting room. A call to come in for the x-ray was next. There was a big yellow sign warning that pregnant women should not take the x-rays. My husband was in the room with me. We agreed that I would let her know that I might be pregnant when the technician came back into the room.

The technician hurried out of the room. The nurse came into the room and asked if I was pregnant. I told her I did not know. I was told to go get a pregnancy test, and if it was negative, I should make an appointment to see the doctor. The nurse said to wait there while she told the doctor. The doctor could be heard cursing all the way down the hallway. The doctor came in to see us and started scolding us right away as if we were little kids that had misbehaved. He told us to get out of his office and go get a pregnancy test. His face was beet red! His loud cursing could be heard even outside.

We did not go get a pregnancy test. I knew the night of conception was the night I came home from the hospital.

There was a different feeling the very next morning. Something was different inside, as if there had been some sort of shift. As the weeks came and went, there were no sickly feelings. The third week after coming out of the hospital meant a trip to the orthopedist. He had warned about falling and not getting pregnant. What if I was pregnant? It would be a miracle, and my crushed pelvis might not support the fetus.

An appointment was made with an obstetrician. It was confirmed we were pregnant for about a month. The obstetrician was concerned that as the baby grew, my womb may not be able to support her. He was optimistic that a cesarean would be the safest way to proceed if we could get to the second trimester. This procedure would ensure the baby would be okay, and so would I. I had always assumed the babies would come naturally. Yes, the goal was to have at least six children. These plans were made before the accident and before the marriage had fizzled like a dying firework.

Knowing that a child had been conceived cast some hope for the marriage to survive. There were no complications throughout the pregnancy. Most days were spent alone, learning to maneuver with the walker and then the walking sticks. The baby seemed to sleep a lot, and therewas only one morning of sickness. The pregnancy was keptsecret from both sets of parents. It did not seem fair to get everyone all excited again. Something could go wrong again.

The weight loss from being in the hospital helped to keep the secret. It was easier to believe that the little weight gain was due to independent eating. The hospital only served healthy, low-calorie meals. It was believed that at home, choices were made that accounted for the weight gain. Some of the outfits worn before the accident actually fit well during the pregnancy. The outfits were loose enough to hide my growing belly.

The pain from bones healing was weathered. The injuries to my face healed very well. There are still a few noticeable scars. The baby could only have vitamins. There could be no pain killers to ease the constant hurting. The pelvis and the left side continued to knit back together. The baby kept growing with no bad side effects.

Five and a half months into the pregnancy, I became quite anxious. It was at this stage the miscarriage had happened. This time it was not about fibroids outgrowing the baby. It was whether my barely knitted pelvic bones could support the weight of a growing fetus. I prayed a lot then, and I still pray a lot even now. I thanked God for giving me a baby and asked Him to protect her. He did, and He does.

* * *

Regular visits to the doctor showed that everything was right on schedule. This baby was a tired little one, sleeping most of the time. The ultrasound showed her sucking her thumb. I was a thumb sucker until the age of eleven, so there was no surprise there. The heartbeat was strong and steady, calming my fears. Although the baby was content to suck her thumb and sleep, I was not.

I wanted strawberries, grapes, ice cream, plums, bananas, oranges, tangerines, and popcorn. Oh yeah, I wanted 7-Eleven slushies. Trips were made in the middle of the night to the all-night vegetable market in Orlando. Of course, once the fruit and other stuff were bought, the thought of eating it was out of the question. Just smelling the strawberries started a queasy feeling deep inside. For the first time in my life, my tooth started aching.

Never had a toothache or cavity in my life; I did not understand how this happened. My husband had experienced toothaches, and so he was sympathetic. I could not have this throbbing pain in my mouth for another minute. It was one o'clock in the morning, and my husband had to be at work at seven-thirty. The thought of hurting this way all day alone was unbearable. He took me to the emergency room. The doctor there referred us to a dentist and made an appointment for eight o'clock the next morning. The next morning my husband called his job to let them know he would be late.

There was no waiting at the dentist. The receptionist got some information from me, including the fact that I was pregnant. The nurse ushered me into the examination room, and the dentist came in. The dentist calmed me and told me it was not unusual for a pregnant woman to have a toothache. He explained that the fetus was pulling the calcium from my body as it grew. The dentist suggested extraction as the tooth was on the side of the mouth. Attempting to fill the cavity would require unknown amounts of painkillers. This could be dangerous for the baby. The extraction would stop the pain, and the space where the tooth was would not be seen. In less than thirty minutes, the tooth was taken out, and we were on the way home. Two days after removing the tooth, there was minimal pain.

The waiting for the arrival of my blessing was nerve-wracking. Waiting can be a hard job. "Patience is a virtue," as the Bible states, was never more obvious than at this time. No matter what the expectant mother wants or does, the baby comes when it is ready. The only exception is in cesarean deliveries. In those cases, a time to remove the baby surgically through the stomach is made in advance.

We lived next door to my parents. Trying to hide the fact that I was pregnant was not hard. Mama only questioned the fact that I did not want more than one of her delicious homemade biscuits. I do not believe she thought I was pregnant. She did think I was getting sick again. Guilty for not telling her, I kept the baby a secret. I had always eaten at least two biscuits with syrup whenever it was possible. Now, the thought of eating one was all I could muster. Most times, I would tell her I was taking them home to eat later. Mama accepted this excuse and would put two more in the foil for my husband.

The first date for delivery was July 10, 1974. The date came and passed with no baby. The next predicted date was July 20th. There was no delivery each week going in for my doctor's appointment. On this date, the doctor said, "well, it is certainly not long now. The waiting is almost over. He said, "The baby has turned and is in position in the birth canal." The word excitement is an understatement of how we felt.

My husband went fishing regularly. He and his best friend would go early Saturday mornings. The best friend had just welcomed a new baby into the world a few weeks earlier. His wife was busy with their now three children, so he was anxious for these times going fishing. My husband was reluctant to leave me home alone this Saturday morning as delivery time was so close. He decided to take me along with him instead of leaving me home by myself. His friend understood and did not come along with us.

I was not interested in going fishing at all. I just wanted the baby to come out. He kept going on about fishing, and so we went. Pelvic pressure was starting as the drive to the fishing spot was begun.

Although never carrying a baby to full term, I knew there was still some time before the baby came. Staying in the car for most of the first couple of hours just laying down, I slept. My husband would come up from the creek bed

* * *

every now and then to check on me. LATER ON, as I got out of the car, I baited my hook. The only thing ever used were live wigglers (worms). The moment my line was cast, something big snatched at the bait. I reeled and pulled, trying to get the thing in closer. My husband came over to help. He reeled the big butter catfish in. To this day, it is the biggest fish I have ever caught. Shortly thereafter, we returned home with my big catch of the day.

After fishing, the first thing on the agenda was to take a shower, then lay down. The contractions were getting stronger and longer. I did not say anything for a while because I knew my husband would panic. I would have to be in the hospital just waiting, knowing it was not quite time yet. Finally, I let him know about the contractions very late in the afternoon. True to form, he wanted to call the doctor and go to the hospital. The call was made to the doctor.

The doctor told him to count the minutes between each contraction. He also told him to ask me how strong the contractions were. A call back to the doctor made him realize there was still some time before leaving for the hospital. The strong contraction woke me up at four-thirty in the morning. I wanted to wait, but my husband insisted we get to the hospital. He did not stop at the 7 Eleven for my Slurpee as I asked him to. That made me very angry. I knew once we got there, there could be no more drinking anything! We arrived at the hospital at six in the morning. The contractions were not any worse, but they were closer together. The water bag had not broken. The nurses and attendants made sure all of us expectant mothers were comfortable. All of us were in a single room with four beds. Each mother's time would come, and they would be wheeled into delivery. I was left there still in labor.

After being in the labor room for six hours, the nurse let me have a tiny cup of crushed ice. I was warned to only suck a little at a time. It was the size cup that medicine was given in. My husband had the nerve to be sitting outside the room waiting. The doctor was puzzled that my labor was going so slow. He decided to burst my water bag. This speeded things up a bit. The time was six o'clock p.m. I had been at the hospital for twelve hours. At seven o'clock, the doctor came in, stated that he was on his way home and that his associate would deliver my baby. The next time the nurse checked, I had dilated to nine centimeters, and the baby's head was in sight.

My doctor's name could be heard as they paged him. The delivery nurse said that he was gone for the day. I was scared. My doctor knew all about me, and I did not want some strange doctor delivering my baby. In all honesty, I had met and been seen by the associate on at least one occasion. My doctor came rushing into the room. He said,

"Aright Mrs. Rouse let's get your baby here!" The doctor told me to push when he said so. I did, and my beautiful little baby girl entered the world at seven-thirty-six p.m.

My little one was still sleepy after the initial slap to the bottom. She put her finger in her mouth and went backto sleep. The nurse laid her on my chest, she peeked at me for a moment and she slept on. All the measuring was done.She weighed six pounds seven ounces. It did not seem as ifshe was that big. Then wrapping her up for her daddy to see, she was taken to the nursery. I called my Mama and excitedly told her that she had a new baby granddaughter named Tamara Lynn. My Mama wanted to know where I was and why she had not seen me all day. In order to convince her that I really did just give birth to my daughter, I put my husband on the phone. She believed him. He told her again what hospital I was in. She wanted to come the next day, but I told her we would be home the day after that.

Mama called me the next morning and laughed about how I had fooled her and Mother (my mother-in-law). One day passed, and then we were on our way home. I went straight into my Mama's house with the baby. My Mama laughed and cried. She said, "You devil you" I did not know. I explained that I knew she was not well and did not want her worrying about me. After all, I had just spent three months in the hospital after the bad car wreck. I was in a wheelchair. I could not walk yet. Mama watched me struggling to walk again. Mama was struggling with diabetes. I learned to walk while I was carrying Tami. It just seemed that she had enough to worry about.

All she could do was look at the little, tiny bundle and hold her close. I felt like she was holding me. There was so much love in her eyes. It was one of the only times I ever saw my daddy get emotional. He just smiled and tried to hide the moisture in his eyes. Finally, he just went outside to sit in the yard. He would cry again when Mama died three years later.

Even though our house was about twenty-five yards from my parents, Mama insisted I should stay there. Mama said I was going to need help with my baby. My husband slept in our house most nights. Me and the baby stayed just a week in the house with Mama and Daddy. The first night in our own house was uneventful. I was breast feeding and so I fed the baby every three hours. This little girl did not cry and fret like some babies do. All she seemed to want was to be full, dry, and close enough to hear my voice.

Going outside to hang some diapers on the line, I placed Tami all the way on the far side of the bed next to the wall. Just to be safe, I placed pillows at her side and feet. It took maybe five minutes to hang the diapers. Tami was only four weeks old, and I had never witnessed her wiggling or trying to turn over. Coming back into the house, I saw that the bed was empty. My heart leaped into my throat, and I almost dropped to the floor. I had a clear line of sight to the door while hanging up the clothes. No one had been in the house. Nothing was out of place, except the baby was not on the bed where I placed her. All kinds of things were going through my head. There was not a sound in the room. My brain finally started to function again. I thought she had fallen behind the bed somehow and was hurt so bad she could not cry. It was the only thing that made any sense. I was too afraid to look. I was too afraid of what I might find.

I got up the nerve to look. There she was, curled up, sleeping where she slid off the bed. I gently picked her up, still scared. She was covered with dust bunnies. She stretched long and hard and went right back to sleep. I stayed on the bed with her all the rest of that day, just gazing at her and thanking God she was fine. She has never left on the bed again. She was introduced to Shaft at two months old.

The shaft was my German shepherd/collie mixed puppy. My husband had gotten him for me when I was in the hospital. Tami and Shaft became inseparable. The shaft was a puppy just as Tami was a baby. He was a smart dog that learned things easily. Shaft decided that his main job was to guard the baby. He was excellent at his job and took it very seriously. If we were outside in the yard, no one could come near Tami. No strangers could get anywhere near her. He would only relax if my husband or me gave him the command that it was okay. Shaft did everything to help when Tami was learning to crawl and walk. At first, being unsteady trying to walk, there was a lot of falling, just like most kids. The shaft would position his body so that Tami could grab his fur and pull herself up. It never seemed to hurt him when she did this.

Shaft fell in love with a girl from the other end of our street. The other end was across highway 419. There were only white families in that neighborhood then. No black family lived in the Sweet Water Park area. Shaft brought his love home one morning. She stayed all day. The shaft went again and again to visit her. The beautiful girl dog was smitten too. At our house, the two of them would run and play. One night he went to visit and never returned.

Searching up and down, we could never find out what happened to him. If he were alive, he would come home.

The only public pool in our town was at Sweet Water Park. The Equal Rights Amendment forced the admission of Blacks into the pool. However, a Hawaiian family moved to town and were accepted as equal. The family had skin darker than many Blacks but had no problems using all public facilities. The bias was for Blacks only. It was a public facility, and everyone should have been allowed to use it. It was the law. The city decided to close the pool rather than admit Blacks. It remained closed for forty-plus years. Separate but equal was often circumvented by the powers in control of the government. Every taxpayer helped fund the pool each time taxes were paid. Another twenty-plus years would pass before a person of color was elected to the city council. Representation was still disproportionate. It was a start.

Mama was willing and anxious to spend as much time as possible with her grandbaby. A search for work was begun. Finding a job at a chain of sandwich shops working in the commissary required standing the entire shift. It was not easy. Although my husband worked and made more than enough to support us, he controlled it all. Not much had changed in that regard since reconciliation.

The new car bought while in the hospital had been recalled. The design had proven to be dangerous, and the gas tanks had to be revised. This meant sharing one car again. It would have made sense for me to drop my husband at work. I could have used the car the entire day while he worked, but that was not satisfactory. This is why I went to work to get another car of my own. I never understood the threat he felt from my desire to be independent. I was willing to try living together again, and our baby's blessing was monumental. I had no understanding of this need to control everything about our lives.

Working at the sandwich shop for six months, it was getting harder to continue this grueling work. Not much money was saved from working. The money was spent on the baby and me. About ready to give up this job, I received an offer to work for the local community organization. I declined. Mama heard of the offer and fussed with me about refusing. Mama and others in the community thought I would be the perfect candidate.

At this time, the realization that the marriage was not going to work was faced. The decision was made to accept the job offer. Our daughter deserved to be raised with happy parents. If this meant happy parents that did not live together, then so be it. I took the job with the community group. This new job took up a lot of time, but there were opportunities to spend time with my baby. From the very beginning, my husband complained about the job.

There were required meetings, fundraisers and provision of services that was my job. The job required me to remain on call twenty-four hours a day. The calls received after regular office hours would usually be handled with referrals to appropriate agencies. Our daughter was fourteen months old. Most of the fundraisers were held on Saturdays. My job was to support the cause however possible. In other words, my physical presence was required at these events.

The fundraisers were always in our town. It never failed. There was never a time my husband would keep our baby without complaining. More than once, he actually brought the baby to me at the fundraiser. Telling me I had been there long enough, he left her and sped away. My job was on the line because of this disruptive nonsense. The separation was coming again. The only way to split was for me to stay in our little house, and he needed to move out.

Finally able to convince him to leave, I was able to concentrate on my job. He had all he needed to get an apartment. He had a car. He certainly was able to afford his own place. The agreement was made that the baby could spend time with him. He loved her as I did. The first time he asked if she could spend the night. I agreed. It was decided that he would bring her to me the next day. Noon the next day, I was waiting anxiously for my baby. At three o'clock, I went to get my daughter because he told me she was not coming back to me on the phone.

Arriving at the complex, I knocked on my husband's door. He talked through the door, telling me to go away that he was keeping our daughter. Using a whole lot of profanity and still not getting my daughter, I finally calmed down. I called the Sheriff's Department. A Deputy arrived at the apartment shortly after that. The deputy convinced him to open the door and turn the baby over to me. Of course, the child was unaware of what was going on and was happy to see me. Being cautioned by the Deputy not to attack him physically, I took the baby and left. I was so thankful she was alright. Clearly, some mental issues were going on with him. What made him think I would go along with my child living with him?

The new job opened a whole new world of possibilities. Being able to concentrate fully on work was freedom for me. As a community outreach worker, this job made it possible to do the things my Mama had taught me. Mama taught me to help someone when they need to arise and to help with a humble heart. Immediately a one-room office was rented for the services that would be provided. The local organization, the Oviedo Citizens in Action, was overseer. Services were accessed by those living within and outside the city limits. It was an amazing opportunity to work in the area to identify and deliver services.

The Federal Community Action Agency was the parent company. This group was a conglomerate of community groups throughout the nation. These non-profits provided many services to families that slipped through the cracks in qualifying for assistance. However, the main focus of the community organization was to keep the public involved in creating change. The vision was to build a community center in the low-income target areas eventually. The voter registration drive is still an ongoing activity for the organization.

Many people of color did not exercise the right to vote. Many more were not registered to cast their vote.

Educating the community on this issue and many others was an everyday challenge. The most disturbing realizationwas that young adults felt as if their vote would not make adifference. It was an uphill battle to change these beliefs. This group of non-voters would participate in the fundraisers and then not go to the polls at election time. As the community came together, this position started to change slowly.

The years started to come and go faster and faster, or so it seemed. Our precious gift, Tami continued to grow up. Entering an early education development program, my little one excelled. My baby was only three years old. Each morning as she marched towards her classroom, I felt like crying. Most of what was taught in the program had already been taught at home. While attending school with others, this little girl caught everything that blew through. Every time a child in the class had a cold or any communicable ailment, she would contract that illness.

Her body would be limp and hot with fever when picked up from school. Her stomach would be upset. The eyes would change during this time. A dullness came in, or a shutter came down over the spark that was usually there. Nothing excited this sickly child. The curriculum at the school was not a challenge for the child. Those days when illness made it wise to keep her with me that is what I did. Taking her into the office with me, her condition was monitored. All of these times, the illness just had to run its course. A trip to the doctor might get a prescription for an antibiotic. Most of the time, the medicine could not stay down. The times when the fever was not under control within twenty-four hours, a trip to the doctor was next.

Looking back on it all, the trips to the pediatrician were more for me than for my child. What I mean is, the doctor would tell me the same thing each time. My little one had just picked up some bug. The doctor advised continually hydrating, limiting milk and milk products, and letting her eat what she wanted. There was no forcing her to eat. She did not want anything. A couple of salted pretzels and a few sips of Pedialyte were enough for an entire morning. A few crackers and more Pedialyte was dinner. The missing school did not affect my daughter's progress there. The interaction with the other children is what was missed the most. Being an only child meant a lot for her to develop social skills.

The early childhood program was for three and four-year-old children. The program was a pre-head start model.

Completion and age progression eventually put the participants in the five-year-old kindergarten class.

Entering kindergarten, or "big" school as it was called, was a ritual. The classes were no challenge once again. It did not warrant skipping a grade, in my opinion. The only thing that made this challenging was being around more children, which guaranteed more sickness spells. Near the middle of my baby's kindergarten year, I found out another baby had started to grow inside me.

The very first person to learn of the pregnancy was my baby girl. Her happiness was contagious, even with the upset stomach I always had. My baby was convinced from the beginning that the baby growing inside me was a girl. I asked how she could be so sure it was a girl, and she said, "because a boy just won't do." The two of us laughed a lot about this. Both of us still laugh now when it comes up in our walk down memory lane. This pregnancy was certainly different.

Throughout the entire pregnancy, this baby was active. It was as if she was doing somersaults inside there! This baby was constantly moving, kicking, and punching. It did not help that nauseous was a constant companion. All of the doctor's checkups showed a healthy regular-sized fetus. So much nauseous made it almost impossible to eat much of anything. Even so, my belly was huge. There was always speculation of whether twins were inside me. The doctor kept checking but could only see one very active little girl.

Another miracle was on the horizon. Since being told no children were in my future, now number two was on the horizon. Maybe this is why hearing the news of having no children did not upset me for too long. Doctors know what they know. There is a higher power than their knowledge. God allowed me to be a parent again.

Parenting does not come with a set of guidelines that apply to each birth. It is learned as you go and follow the positive examples of good parents in your circle. A good parent wants to do everything right. This usually does not happen. The fact is, while planning is taking place, the plan has been put in place from the time of conception. Twenty-nine is not a wise age yet. There are still so many things to learn. One thing to relearn is that babies come when they are good and ready to.

This baby was no exception. The doctor predicted October 7 as the due date. The seventh rolled right on past with no sign of delivery. The next approximate date was the

14th of October. Once again, no delivery or even labor on that date. The morning of October 18 was bright and warm. The baby was doing jumping jacks or some such thing inside me. By nine o'clock, the contractions had started.

I called my sister to come to take me to the hospital. None of the stuff my sister asked me had happened. My water had not broken, the contractions were not ten minutes apart. The contractions were not frequent, but they were painful.

My sister agreed it would be wise to get to the hospital. This was dejavu. This woman would not stop to get a drink for me. The anger started to escalate with the pain of the contractions. There was no reason why a short stop at the 7-11 could not happen! It was on the same road to the hospital, only thirty minutes from home. The agreement was to leave me there while she went to work and then come back after work to check on me.

Laying there in labor with constant nausea, I asked for some ice chips. The nurse did not hesitate and brought me a small cup. That nurse would have brought me anything I asked for if I would just stop throwing up. The nurses were amazed I was regurgitating so close to delivery.

Their conversation could be heard as they talked among themselves. They kept saying it had never happened on their watch. Four hours passed, and dilation was only at four and a half. The cervix had to open for the baby to come down the birth canal safely. Ten centimeters is considered perfect for the mother to start pushing to help the baby get outside the mother's body. The doctor came in again, looked, and was satisfied all was well. While he was there in the room with me, I threw up again.

The next time the doctor came at six o'clock. The doctor talked about speeding up the labor. My desire to deliver was attached to my sickly stomach. The doctor did give me something intravenously that sped up labor. After the water bag broke, the baby was on the move. Just after nine o'clock on October 18, 1979, Selena Kerise came into the world. The nurse brought her to me. This little beauty was so pale that she looked like a white child! Being awake throughout the delivery, there was no thought that maybe this was the wrong baby! After her initial scream of protest at having her bottom swatted, she stuck her finger in her mouth. This cutie stared at me a minute, then went to sleep.

Her head was covered with very long hair that just laid flat against her scalp. The doctor said all that hair was probably the reason for my nausea during the pregnancy. This was a new age in giving birth. The baby was brought right into the room with me. It was my choice to keep her there with me or have her stay in the nursery. Choosing to have her with me, we snuggled up together. After all that mixing up inside me, Selena was perfectly still. She looked like a little sleeping doll. Her skin was so fair and her hair so straight. The hospital staff could hardly believe she was mine when the nursing shift changed.

I suppose my very dark skin and my very light-skinned baby just did not match up in their minds. They could not hide the surprised look on their faces when checking on us for the first time. This reaction had me anxious, and I did not want them to take her from the room for any reason. There are mean people everywhere.

My oldest daughter's dad brought her to see hersister. Technically he was still my husband. He knew the baby was not his. This must-have confused the staff even more. He was not as dark-skinned as I, but he was nowherenear the skin color of my baby. My oldest, Tamara, was justfive years old but was very wise. She looked at the baby andsaid, "Selena, you're here." I told her that I had not named the baby yet. She told me the baby was named Selena. Her class had been reading a story about a little Mexican girl named Selena. She liked the name, and I thought it was pretty. That night I named her Selena Kerise.

I breastfed Tamara and intended to breastfeed my baby. This beautiful new baby did not nurse well. The nurses assured me that some babies take longer to start feeding on the mother's breast. As the breast begins to produce milk, they hurt if they are not suckled or drained by hand. My baby was fed formula in a bottle every other scheduled feeding. By the time of our release from the hospital, she was nursing well.

Somehow, I got a cold and so decided to bottle feed Selena until the cold had run its course. These alternate bottles of formula did not stay in her stomach. One day turned into two. The baby was only drinking a couple of ounces of milk at each feeding. The pediatrician was called and thought that these symptoms warranted an office visit. The same doctor taking care of my firstborn was also taking care of my newborn. My baby was just two weeks old.

The doctor said that my baby had pneumonia. This scared me so much. She assured me that with treatment, my tiny baby would be okay. The doctor thought the baby was healthy otherwise but might be allergic to milk from cows. That day the doctor gave me three cans of soy isolate formula to feed Selena. It is milk made from soybeans. She did not like this either but did not throw it back up. If this milk was not thrown up, then the baby could be fed this soy milk as an alternative to milk from cows.

The medicines prescribed by the doctor had me and the baby feeling good in a few days. Later tests revealed that my baby was allergic to cow's milk and all the stuff made with that milk. Some form of milk is in most things consumed by us. The constant watch over what my baby was fed became just another part of being a good mom. The few times a babysitter was needed, that person had to be reminded about the allergy to milk and milk products. During the time of bottle feeding, it was not so hard to control what my baby was fed. The advance to solid food made it harder. Even so, as a toddler, control of her diet was maintained better than later on when she started school.

There was never a shortage of babysitter possibilities. One of my favorite nieces was my first choice. This sweet girl had been there to take care of my firstborn whenever I needed her. There was not a lot of need for a babysitter because Mama was right next door. Mama was always ready and willing to keep/watch Tamara. She had already passed on before my youngest was born.

My niece, Ann, would walk a good distance to just see and play with my babies. She was in her early teen years. I trusted her totally with the girls and have never regretted leaving them with her for any amount of time. There was complete trust in her love for my babies. Some- times I did not need a babysitter, but she would still come and just be with us. The girls and me loved having her with us.

A small child that relies on its mother to give it food can be kept safe from things that could make the child sick. The moment the child starts crawling, then walking, the job of control is more intense. Natural curiosity develops faster and faster as they grow up.

The first time my baby knew that rolling and twisting helped her change positions, it was a whole new ball game. Putting up a fort of pillows did not work. Somehow this wiggler managed to get over and through the fort. One day, this one wiggled under the bed and decided dust bunnies were playmates. It was dark under there, but she was not afraid. Grabbing her foot to pull her from underneath the bed made her giggle out loud. Pulling her out, she was covered in lint and happy about it. The lint in her hair was the worst and the hardest to get out. Washing her soft, fine hair was the only way to get this mess out of her hair!

It was so hard to explain why she could not have ice cream to a two-year-old. There was sherbert at our house. Although it looked like ice cream, it was made from fruit. Once this child entered school, it was a major game-changer. The health card showed the allergy, the teachers were told of the condition. The school meals often included milk and milk products. Preparing a bag lunch was the perfect solution. The child would still get sick with stomach problems regularly. It was a sign that some milk product had been ingested.

● ● ●

The careful oversight was not working as the children traded lunch items. For a three-year-old, an Oreo cookie is a major treat and worth getting sick to have one. Even now, this child rationalizes eating some form of milk or milk product and just loves ice cream. Whenever mac and cheese, cake, or ice cream is eaten, it will make her sick. The doctor thought that growing older would make a difference like some children. This child did not grow out of this allergy. No milkshakes for her without paying the price.

Public schools were open nine months of each year. The return to school always commenced on the Tuesday after Labor Day. My days with the girls and at work were intertwined. Unless there was some job-related reason to travel, the girls went to work with me. The actual offices of the community organization were approximately 100 yards from where we lived. The land the group purchased was close to the property daddy owned and where I lived. Being blessed with many nieces and nephews, there was no problem finding a babysitter. These young people would volunteer. My job must have looked glamorous to them, and to spend time with the girls and me was special. Before a grant was found to hire young staff from the high school, these teenagers helped. These teens would pass out flyers and put-up posters throughout the service area to help make my job easier.

The funding for the parent organization that paid my salary was in jeopardy. The relationship with the father of my youngest was also becoming more troublesome. A few months before funding ran out, a decision was made to relocate to the place where I was born. This was a tough decision to make. The choices were to stay and be miserable or leave the state and return to the place of my birth.

There was never a thought that relocating was going to be easy with a five-year-old and an eight-month-old baby.

The actual move was a sort of test run. The test was three weeks. The family would stay with my oldest sister and herfamily for three weeks. During that time, I would look foremployment. A lot happened in those three weeks.

The night before a job interview, no one could find the iron. The blouse and skirt chosen to wear were both horribly wrinkled. I knew I could not show up like that on the morning of the interview. My brother came to pick me up, and I asked him to take me apartment hunting instead. He took me to three places, none of which had any openings. My name was placed on the waiting lists of each apartment complex. Returning to the island where my sister lived, my brother passed by the road that would take us back there. Just riding and talking for a while, I saw this sign that said, "FOR RENT."

Writing the number down on a piece of paper, the excitement returned. That evening a call was made to the number on the sign. The lady told me the place was not ready and needed a lot of repairs. After listening to my situation, this lady gave me her cousin's phone number. This cousin lived further down on the island but had rented places by the week. At this time, my money was very low.

There were only about thirty dollars in cash and twenty-sixdollars in food stamps.

I made the call to the number the lady had given me. A very educated-sounding voice answered the phone. Explaining my situation to this stranger, I became emotional. The lady told me that she only had a single room available. The cost was twenty-six dollars per week, and rooms were not rented to women! Explaining to her that I had a five-year-old and a baby eight months and just needed a place of my own for a few months.

The Lord must have changed her heart because she told me to come to see the room after a while on the phone. This lady further explained that one of the people living in the rooming house was her godson. The other was an older man that worked for the state, and he drank a lot. It was decided that the room could be seen the next day at one o'clock. Upon my arrival, the address was a two-story cinder-block building. This perspective landlady lived upstairs.

One of the young teenagers saw me struggling to get to the steps and asked who it was I was there to see. Once Iexplained, this girl went up the stairs and told this lady I hadcome to see the room. The girl told me to just wait downstairs as the lady, Harriett, would come down to show me the room. This was a teenaged girl, and she called this lady by her first name. A short while later, a small gray-haired lady came out of the apartment upstairs and locked the door behind her. The little lady introduced herself as

Harriett Scott. I introduced myself and my children. My oldest very politely said, "how do you do," my baby was just happy and giggling.

Mrs. Harriett was so impressed by the good manners of Tamara and commented that I must have been teaching her well!

The lady told me to come with her around to the next building. While walking there, the lady commented that my child was trained well and asked her age. There was also a comment made about how well my daughter spoke. As we neared the rooming house, the lady stated once again that she did not rent to women. I told her that we would be moving out the moment I found a job and a place. As in all rooming houses, the bathroom and kitchen are shared. This lady scolded me that a rooming house was no place for children. I suppose she had decided to give me a chance. I was told to come the next day to give her a chance to deep clean the bathroom and kitchen. I volunteered to come clean, but the lady straightened me out. She stated that the place should be cleaned upon renting, and she would see to it that it was. I asked when I should pay the rent. I was told rent was due on Friday evenings. It was Tuesday.

The girls and me moved in the very next day. I had cleaned the room thoroughly. The bed was big enough for us. It was the end of June, and it was so hot in that room. Using cardboard to keep the girls fanned was hard to sleep. The lady refused to take my rent money the first week. It was enough for her that I just took care of my children.

• • •

Later on, someone told me that she had never had children of her own but had raised many. This was just like my Mama had done! Mama was known to have raised lots of children but had never given birth to any.

As it turned out, everyone in that general area was related in some way. Everyone that is except me. Still, my children and I were accepted and treated well. The fact that this lady had rented me a room amazed them all. People would say that the lady must really like me a lot, stating that not even female family members could rent a room there. This landlady explained to me that a few females had been given a chance to stay there. Each time it did not work out for various reasons. Her favorite word was that even though the women had been family, they were "trifling." The word was not used much where I was raised, but the meaning was clear. It meant a person that did not handle their affairs well.

It was hard to find a job without a car to search around and get to the job. There was no publictransportation on any part of the island just yet. It would take three more years before the Emmanuel Missionary Baptist Church bought a bus. The church started a daily bus service to downtown. The bus went to Folly Beach, designated spots on James Island, and then downtown. Everyone appreciated this service. The church-supported bus service did not serve any of the other barrier Islands. Riders on the church bus were all races and colors. Whoever had the bus fare was able to ride.

The first so-called job I had was created from necessity. While preparing dinner for my girls and me, the rooming house neighbor commented on how great it smelled. The neighbor was offered a plate. He eagerly accepted the food. The next day this neighbor asked me to cook dinner Monday through Friday each week, and he would pay for his meals. A price was agreed upon. The first meal served was pork chops, fried cabbage, white rice, and cornbread. The entire time he lived there, his dinner was cooked in the kitchen there. This lasted for six weeks. The man always paid his bill and even gave me rides to the store. He drank a lot but was neat and clean. The landlady evicted him shortly after we moved in.

Living there in the rooming house for just a few days, a lady came around to the front of the porch. This lady introduced herself, and a friendship started that lasted until her death thirty-five years later. My new friend fell in love with my babies. She and her husband had nine children. All nine of these children still lived at home. However, four were grownups. Three already had children of their own. Dinner at their house was cooked in huge pots and pans. There were a lot of mouths to feed. A lot of family in one small house was not strange to me. It was almost identical to my beginning so long ago. None of my older brothers and sisters had children. A few were old enough to be my parent.

My new friend worked two part-time jobs. The first job was cleaning the house for a white family in the mornings. Most days, she would come home at one o'clock. At three o'clock in the afternoons, my friend cleaned the elementary school. This was done each day, Monday through Friday. It seemed as if my friend was always washing clothes, cooking or cleaning. The weariness could be seen in her eyes. She never complained. My constant search for work was unsuccessful. There was no transportation to the few jobs that were offered.

My friend tried to get a job for me cleaning the schools. There were no openings. The workers that had these jobs had been doing them for years. During the summers, many people made money by working on the farms. There was plenty of work on this island and the other islands for a few weeks. Farming was still a decent way to make a living even in the early 1980s. This friend encouraged me to go with her to the farms. The closest I had come to any farm work was picking oranges off my daddy's trees in our backyard! Even so, most of those were eaten. The only other experience with farm work was, helping my grandaddy weed his garden at our house when I was a little girl.

Years earlier, some young adult friends had convinced me to go on the bus to the tobacco picking fieldsone week. My friends talked about how much fun they hadon the bus trip to and from the farms. Since there were no children to consider yet, I decided to go with them. It took two hours to get to the tobacco farm and two hours for thereturn trip home. By twelve o'clock, the heat and the tiredness had all but made me a defeated lump. All-day longin that blazing hot Florida sun, I made $8.75! I was angry and so painful from reaching down to pick the plants. I never did any farm work again until years later while living on the Island.

The landlady had accepted rent for one week. The room had been ours for three weeks. Not knowing where the rent money was coming from for the next week, I went on the farm with my new friend. I was afraid when I rode in the back of a pickup truck with a camper on it. Certain that the man taking us to the farm would know that I did not know anything about this work. I thought I would be fired. The first job our crew had was to put in tomato stakes. Tomato stakes are the poles the tomato plant climbs up as the plant grows. There were two jobs. Jab the wooden stakes into the ground or walk-behind and hammer them into the dirt. The hammers were heavy, but the stakes had to be carried in the arms of those pushing them down. Knowing I was not as coordinated as some, I chose to be a hammer. After a couple of hours of this tedious work, our clothes were soaking wet. Finally, it was lunchtime. Finding whatever little shade there was, we sat down in the dirt and ate our lunch. Sweat was pouring off of me. I was so miserable out there. During lunch, my friend encouraged me to hang in there. In a short while, it was time to go back to work. As the day came to an end, all of us were drained. I vowed never to come on the farm again, even though there was no other job.

On the way home, I inquired about our pay. Apparently, twenty-three dollars a day was the going rate for this type of work. It was nineteen eighty. My children were at my friends' house. Her older daughter was babysitting. I had worried all day long about my girls while my friend assured me they were well taken care of. The boss stopped everywhere on our way home. The thirty-minute drive took two hours. My friend was finally showing some sign of tiredness. My children were happy to see me, and I was so happy to see them.

The children had been bathed and fed. My babysitter helped me get them to the rooming house. It was only thirty or forty yards from where my friend lived. The man still living in the rooming house had taken a bath and left the tub filthy. Covered with dirt and sweat, I had to clean and disinfect that tub before cleaning myself. Afterward, eating a peanut butter and jelly sandwich, I fell asleep as soon as it was finished. The girls had both gone to sleep.

The use of an alarm clock was a luxury that could not be afforded. Although going to sleep so tired, my body awoke early as usual. Early the next morning, my friend came to see if I was going to work that day. I got dressed, took my girls to the babysitter, and went to meet the work truck. Surviving one day encouraged me to try again. My calculations came to one hundred and fifteen dollars for five days' work. It was not what was paid for social work but sure beat having no pay. This job lasted one and a half more day. That Friday, my pay envelope was correct. I paid the landlady a week's rent and had some money left. The landlady was surprised to hear about the farm work. She said I did not seem cut out for that kind of work. That was a true statement.

There was no farm work for my friend and me. Two of her sons were brick masons. One of the sons talked to his boss about hiring a helper. The boss hired me to help dig foundations, mix mortar and keep the bricklayers supplied with bricks. Those buckets of mortar and those bricks are heavy. Lifting these to the scaffolds set for the second level is even harder. The job paid thirty-two dollars a day! It was possible to take a few breaks during the day, unlike the farm work. The boss found out I had a valid driver's license and would send me on errands to pick up supplies. The bricklayers taught me to lay a windowsill with brick. Cars passing by would often stop and stare at me doing this type of work. This was considered work for men, and it was quite rare to see a woman doing this work!

By this time, the women in the neighborhood warmed up to me. The fact that I was working doing masonry work amazed these women. Apparently, no such thing had ever happened in the world they lived in. No woman they knew had ever done this sort of work. Just likeany other job, the work fizzled out. The same rules applied,last to come, first to go. I learned a lot and was able to buy school clothes and pay school fees.

A retired contractor born and raised in the area heard of a woman's work in construction. This man was in his mid to late seventies when we met. In our first meeting, a pint of liquor was shared, no chaser, just water. The man talked to me about the place where we sat and drank. The very spot, Honeyhill, had been the site of one of the first battles of the civil war! Small, somewhat shallow impressions were pointed out to me. These were called batteries. It was a place with so much history. This history is only mentioned in two or three sentences in public school history books. The rooming house sat on land that held secrets for hundreds of years. There was talk of the souls of dead soldiers still roaming around the area. Once my fear was obvious, the man offered me a job.

The man had a family member that asked him to adda big room to the back of his house. This contractor told me that he only needed one other person to help him.Asked if I thought I could handle the job, I accepted it immediately. Thank you, Lord. This work would last for two weeks and provide a means to take care of my girls. Thenext morning as the contractor rounded the corner of the building, I was waiting. The room was being added to a house just fifteen feet from where I lived. No ride was needed. Once again, the Master had made a way out of no way.

The first task was to dig the foundation for the new room. The contractor and me started digging that morning. This was to be a large room. It took almost three days to dig that foundation. The only experience I had doing manual labor for pay was the farm work and the construction helper. At the end of each day, my body felt broken in many places. Every part of me hurt. A drink with the boss helped to relax me. Upon completion of the foundation, the man ordered the concrete to be delivered that Monday. The weekend was here. The boss bought our lunch from a cousin that sold dinners every Friday. We had fried chicken, red rice, macaroni and cheese, cabbage, and cornbread.

Monday morning came quickly. The babysitter came to the house and took the children with her. This gave me time to have a cup of coffee. The concrete was delivered on time. Several men had heard of the lady helping to build the new addition. Some were there that morning trying to get work for that day. My boss turned them down. He said the only two helpers we would need are an electrician and a carpenter. These men did not leave the job site. It was more entertaining to watch me work. The boss praised my work. This annoyed some of the guys. Although it was not clear what was being said, it was clear that the comments were negative. A lot of snickering went on. As we continued working and ignoring them, the group decided to move on.

The cinder blocks were delivered early the next morning. When the boss got there, the wall construction was begun. My job was to mix the mortar, keep the work area clear of debris and make sure the blocks were within reach of the masons. The blocks are heavy, but I did not complain. The thirty-two dollars guaranteed for each day was incentive enough to suck it up. The contractor was old and drank steadily. Another man was hired to help lay the blocks. Once the blocks were laid, this job would be over for me. Two more days passed, and then my job was finished.

My children were happy. There was no way for them to know how much of a struggle was going on. My baby was eating more solid foods, but still, both had to have milk. The baby did not like the soy milk. It was much more expensive than regular milk. I made sure to buy it to supply the same nutrients as the milk from cows. My little one was only ten months old. It was almost time for school to start for the oldest.

My oldest child would go to elementary school. Tami was enrolled in what was considered one of the best schools. Still much smaller than her peers, she marched to the bus stop like a pro. There were other children going to the bus too, but I went anyway. Selena struggling to get out of my arms to go with her sister, started crying when the bus pulled off. She cried her little self to sleep. I cried too. My

baby was gone off into the big wide world without me, and she was happy about it! The day dragged on. We still lived in the rooming house. The room, bathroom, and kitchen were spotless. The baby and me sat on the porch for hoursuntil it was just too hot outside. Eventually, we went insideand took naps.

Finally, the bus came to bring the children home. The bus stop was about a quarter of a mile from where the house was. My babysitter had to get her little boy and so would get my daughter at the same time. I do not know who was happier to see Tami, me, or Selena. Tami was probably glad to get out of the room for school. A lot of time was spent in the room. There was no trust built up with the neighbors yet. The girls would not be left outside without supervision for more than a moment. Perhaps I was overprotective. If so, then I was guilty. These people were essentially strangers to us. My children are my most precious gifts. Although bad things may happen, it was not going to happen because I was not being careful. Tami excelled in school. The move from the rooming house came two months later. Our time spent there were four months.

That old saying, "It's not what you know but who you know," is usually right. The apartment was only a quarter of a mile from the rooming house. The new landlord was the godson of the lady that owned the rooming house. Just when it looked as if another month would be spent there, we moved into our new apartment. There was no furniture. It was brand new. The cousin of the former landlady gave me a mattress and box spring. It was big enough for us all to sleep on but, it was really for the girls. Plans were made to return to Florida to retrieve the furniture and our other belongings that were left there.

Of course, the best-made plans do not unfold the way it is imagined. The truck was rented with the idea that daybreak would start the journey. The girls were very excited about riding in the big truck with me driving. My brother had been notified of our expected arrival. Eight hours later, we made it there. Pulling into the yard with the fourteen-foot rental truck, to my surprise, a family was living in our Mom and Dad's house. Not only were they living in the house, but they were using my stuff. There was some obvious damage to many pieces. This hurt.

This family had rented the house with my stuff still in it. The rest of my things were in the open-ended garage. Most of the things in the garage were destroyed. Most of the destruction was from moisture. A lot of pieces had mold and mildew. There was no salvaging these pieces. The family in the house was not to blame. This family was well known to us. They had moved in thinking everything in the house belonged to my brother.

My brother saw no wrong in what he had done. Taking the living room, dining room set and some pieces of clothing, the truck was loaded for the return trip. Every dining chair had a slit down the center of the back. I felt covering the back with pillowcases would hide the cuts. It worked. Refusing to argue any more with my brother, I used my energy to get the truck loaded. Ending the argument with a promise to take him to court, we left. Sleep had to be a part of the schedule in order to get us safely back to South Carolina.

My sister-in-law volunteered to ride back with me to help with the children. A six-hour nap revived me. The return trip was without problems. The biggest problem was getting the truck unloaded and returned before the deadline. The guys I had asked to help unload the truck were waiting at the apartment. The deadline was made, and my sister-in-law was on the bus the next morning at five a.m. It was December thirtieth; there was no school. I slept through the night. My sister-in-law made it home to her family to bring in the new year.

In second grade, Tami was placed in the gifted student program at her elementary school. The group had only two students of color. The rest was a mix of Caucasianboys and girls. The school was disproportionately white. Many more blacks could attend this school. Lots of parentswanted their children to go to schools with a high enrollment of blacks and more black teachers. It was a position that was understood. For me, the best learning environment was when I attended an all-black school. I didnot change my daughter's school but stayed informed of what went on by participating in PTA and other groups.

This sounds like an endorsement of segregation or a separate but equal mentality. It is not that. It is a first-hand experience of identifying with educators, students, and staff that was black like us. Attending a segregated school until ninth grade was special. There was so much teaching that was not in those raggedy textbooks. Most of those teachers genuinely cared about us. It would be the best schooling I would ever have. There was never going to be any fair separate, but equal system. The system had to be changed. It did change slowly.

Integration placed black children at the mercy of amped-up, sly racism. There were no black teachers or administrators in the formally all-white schools in those first few years. A black child that was not a brilliant student or a talented sports athlete was invisible. These children were only visible when it came to racist treatment. There were counselors, of course. Somehow these incidents of complaints wound up being the fault of the victim. In all fairness, parents of Black children and community leaders would take up causes of ill-treatment when warranted. The churches in the Black community always stayed involved locally and nationally. This did not help with the day-to-day on-campus life. Most student bodies were five percent black that first year.

Change is scary for everyone involved. Sometimes an entire day would go by without seeing another black student. One had to be very confident and capable or blend into the background. Some teachers would not miss an opportunity to belittle a student or make some snide remark. In all fairness, there were some teachers that treated black students fairly. The cafeteria had a jukebox in the corner. Students could pay a quarter and hear two selections. It never failed; when a black student would choose something, other students acted as if some disease had been passed on to them. The only selections on the thing worth listening to, was the Beatles records.

When my daughter went to school, all public schools had been integrated for years all those years. Our generation lived the civil rights movement. The next generation had to be taught about the movement. After that, it is still hard for the generation to imagine restrictions on people of color. The burden of truth lies with the parents educating their children at home on what is not in those history books. The truth being that Blacks are treated as less than whites in these United States. The laws changed, but the mentality did not for many whites or blacks. Parents tried too hard to shield their children from the real truth of living in the United States of America. Hiding the truth does not change the truth. It will equip a generation of facts and tools for survival. When prejudice rears its ugly head, the children are bewildered. Parents must then go back in time to a place where they fought so hard to leave.

This place is filled with hurt, loss, and bewilderment for many. The decision to protect the children from injustices is lost, as the world, they live in is a constant reminder. Under-standing that this need to shield is out of love, it has them unarmed. The fault lies with successive generations not knowing and therefore unable to teach their children. Parents are a child's first teacher. A child's education should never be limited to the seven hours of instruction given at school. The hours before and after school are crucial in development. The morning and evening rituals are as important as a child's daily instructions in school.

Talking to each other as preparations are made for the day is crucial. Feeding the body, mind, and soul is the most important meal of the day. Once outside the protected nucleus of the family, the real world explodes all around us.

* * *

It is hard for adults. Imagine how much harder it is for a child. The foundation of good families is God first. Taking that first breath in the morning is reason enough to say thank you to the Creator. A conscious effort must be made for the children to understand who they are and where they came from. Only then will a child get a clue of what achievements are possible in their lives.

The end of the school day brings children home. Lessons are being taught as interaction with other family members takes place. Doing chores and finishing homework rounds out the day. The ideal finish for the day would be supper shared around the table with everyone sitting there. This time of being together is appreciated even if scorned by the children. It gives everyone an opportunity to say what is on their minds. The cleanup, bath, and getting clothes ready for the next day is the final chore before prayers and bedtime.

There is always room in the day to dream big. Whether a story jars it in a book or a story in one's head, dream large and in color. For me, escape to other places was accomplished by reading. Mama could read quite well, but daddy could not. It was odd that Daddy could read the Bible very well. He could choose scriptures to lead devotion at church with no problem. There is a memory of him going over the scripture many times on Saturday before it was read in church on Sunday mornings. He had only finished the second grade in school. Mama had finished the seventh grade. Maybe he memorized those scriptures.

Although Daddy was not formally educated, his entrepreneurship was astonishing. Working hard and appreciating the value of a dollar was the key to prospering. Looking back on it, daddy must have constantly been figuring ways to make money. In between long construction jobs, Daddy would find day jobs. Some jobs would last a day; some would last a week. He was always working. A child of the times was to be seen and not heard. A lot was learned from being almost invisible. One day without work and Daddy would become anxious. Mama tried to soothe him, but he just needed to be working.

There was no choice for my brother and me. The examples of working hard, praying hard, and helping others were key in our upbringing. Later in life, it served us both well. Hard work never hurt anybody; at least it did not hurt forever. Mama and Daddy were considered well off. That did not entitle us to a free ride. There was no flashing money or showing off items many could not afford. The only thing that comes to mind is the purchase of a new car every three to four years. That was not showing off, though; it was a necessity. Certain things were expected of us with no bargaining chips. Working for whatever it is we thought we wanted was one of these things. If there was something we wished for, working to pay for it was the only way to get it. Approval had to be granted beforehand. Decisions concerning any actions by any member of the family were discussed and agreed upon. This agreement was between the adults (parents), not the children. It served to remind us that hard work and determination pay off.

These lessons of perseverance were passed down to the following generation. As the world is in constant turmoil, many things remain the same. The inequality of treatment for different races, people of color has continued. However disguised, some might say it has increased. Thankfully, some are unafraid to speak up against the injustices perpetrated here in America. Once again, the previous generation must enlighten our children.

By the time my second child was starting school. There was a new dynamic laced with technology. The percentage of black educators in the classrooms was lower still than those of whites. The reasons for this are varied. Most states did not pay an appealing salary to teachers. Consequently, college graduates decided to pursue careers paying much more than what was offered.

Entire families were more inclined to migrate north for better wages. Lots of graduates entered the field of technology. This was a smart move because this field was guaranteed to stick around. It was a fast track for advancement within the field. Selena was trained in a school where children used computers in their daily learning. About this same time, the newest child abuse laws were passed. Praying was taken out of the schools. The mention is made here because it is the sequence of how things unfolded. Calculators were a must for every student. School districts and states decided to skip the actual processes in math. It was as though a decision was made to cripple the children's thought and reasoning abilities. How one arrives at a solution is as important as the solution. Years have proven this to be true. It became more important for children to excel at operating gadgets than to use the brain to come with solutions.

School for Selena came with a different set of problems. The allergy to milk and milk products was almost as bad as her wandering mind. The medical information sheet for students is either read, filed, then forgotten, or simply ignored. Honestly, it was not all the fault of the teachers. This child of mine became quite the expert at maneuvering around the rules that controlled her allergy to milk and milk products.

My child would get sick regularly while attending school. Trading her lunch was easy. In fairness, the teachers were not all to blame. It was most likely impossible to monitor twenty-five children every moment at lunchtime. Trading lunch was nothing new. This child did not outgrow this allergy as the doctor, and I had hoped.

Today the evidence of ingesting milk and milk products is apparent whenever these foods are consumed. The wonderful taste of those things outweighed the consequences of eating something with milk in it. Eating ice cream was one of the true triggers. It is made of milk, cream, and sugar. My baby would rather have that horrible stomachache than pass on a good scoop of ice cream.

* * *

The new child abuse laws had children threatening parents. When disciplined, some children would talk about calling social services to report mistreatment. Along with the child abuse hotlines, there has always been a parent abuse hotline. The girls might have thought about calling somebody on me, but they never let me hear it. Honestly, the Lord always made way for me to take care of the girls. My love for them was clearly demonstrated each and every day. There were some whippings along the way. Everything was not solved with a switch or belt. Punishments and restrictions were also used. It was not that fear of me that kept them from calling. I believed that breaking the rules required punishment to be determined by me.

As in most families, the oldest was in charge of the younger ones without parents. It was the same in my family. Imagine the surprise when my oldest called me at work to inform me that the youngest had set a fire under the sofa. The fire had been put out. I raced home from work. The house smelled like burning paper or cloth. Questioning my baby girl was going nowhere. Knowing there was no reason to set the fire, the question remained, "why?" Why did she do this? The child was told to go get a switch from the yard. Trying to look contrite or maybe just scared, the girl gave me a little limp switch. Going outside to get my own switch, I continued fussing. The new living room set had been delivered a week ago. Payments had to be made for fourteen months. It was a brand new, beautiful set. There was a sofa, loveseat, glass insert end, and coffee tables. It came with two beautiful lamps. Cooling down for a while, It was time to punish this child. I made it a point not to give punishment when I was angry.

The moment the switching started, that girl tried grabbing the switch. When that did not work, the child dropped to the floor. Dropping to the floor was a classic move passed down through the ages. Once the switch broke, the fly swatter was mangled, and the little cheap metal-handled dollar store broom was destroyed. Going into my room, the "do not disturb" was hung on my doorknob. Hearing her crying, I continued crying too. The house could have burned down. A few days earlier, the oldest had been caught skipping school. I threatened to call the Department of Social Services to have them removed and taken into custody. It was just too much. If I could not trust them, maybe I could save them from themselves. Of course, it was just an empty threat. I still felt that I could take better care of them than anyone else. I loved them but I needed help. I called the Parent Abuse Hotline instead.

The counselor that answered the phone listened to my story. Some questions were asked. Questions like, "Is the child bleeding?" The answer was no. "Are there any cuts or bruises?" There were a few welts but no cuts. The conversation continued for several minutes. The counselor stated that my actions seemed understandable considering the situation. Although the agency did not approve of corporal punishment, the situation did not appear to be child abuse. In the end, the counselor complimented me on my parenting. The man encouraged me to call the hotline any time of day or night. While on the phone, I knew the girls were listening. It helped to be able to vent my frustrations and anxiety. My mind kept going back to the fire under the sofa and imagining what could have happened. Thank God all that happened was a dark spot under the sofa and a stinking smell for a day or two.

The next morning the youngest was dragging around close to the time the bus was scheduled to pick her up. Unable to figure out what the problem was, she was told to get outside to the bus stop. It was right in front of our house. Dragging to the door, my daughter turned her face to reveal a two-inch scratch along her jaw. The child then asked me what she should say if the teacher asked her about the scratch. I told her to tell the teacher that she set a fire under the couch and got spanked for it. While she was trying to avoid the spanking, she dropped to the floor, and the switch caught the side of her face. The child was told that if the teacher had any questions after that, then she could call me at my job at (843) 588-----. The bus came and picked her up. All-day nervousness ruled me. The call never came. The teacher did ask, and the child told her what happened. Nothing else was said.

The girls are five years apart in ages. There was one child in elementary school and one in middle school. Although the youngest is smart, her concentration is short-lived. Testing did not show the need for control medicines at the time. A combination of school district testing and personal physician testing was done. There were no issues of competency. Ritalin was the choice of control drugs in this time period. Some children would appear almost comatose on the Ritalin. Daydreaming was already a problem, so that was not something my child was going to be given. As my baby grew up, this inability to focus continued to be a problem for her. Teacher-student conferences in every grade were the norm. It was always the same conversation of how competent this child was, as if she would just apply herself. She was always talking too much, playing or fighting. Homework assignments were not completed or left at home. The child would leave the house with the assignment and then leave it on the bus. The lack of organization skills was a huge deal. Tablets, binders, books, and loose papers were always just stuffed into the book bag.

Once the oldest graduated high school, the moveback to Florida was set in motion. This move was planned and meant to be a happy time. The child that had just graduated from high school insisted on staying in South Carolina. She planned to find a place to move with her boyfriend. There was no convincing the child to come with us, and in a few days she would be eighteen. Insisting that if she was forced to go for twelve days, her return would happen the moment she reached her eighteenth birthday, insisting that the ticket would be bought as soon as she reached her eighteenth birthday. It did not matter what I said. I gave the child my Buick skylark that was in good condition, and left the next morning. I had made her promise to keep in touch, and our family would stay in touch with her. The rental truck contained all our possessions. The plan was to marry my baby girl's daddy.

Moving out of one house and into another within twenty-four hours was exhausting. The eight-hour drive to the new house was tiring as well. All of us were so excited about this reuniting. Our daughter lived with me in another state for the first twelve years of her life. The only time spent with her dad was a few visits during summer vacation each year. Some years the girls and me would spend the Christmas holidays in Florida. My daughter would see her dad at these times. Although we had never lived under the same roof before, it was agreed that it was time to try.

My baby girl had an older sister that lived nearby. This beauty was already a teen mom and a straight-A student about to finish the eleventh grade. She came to visit one day and shortly thereafter moved in with us. A happy little baby boy was in the house now. This child had a job and took very good care of her son. She worked after schoo and on weekends. Our relationship today is still as good as it was during this time. The only dark cloud was the fact that these girls' Daddy drank too much. He had also started slipping back to the drugs that controlled him. Just a few months into the new arrangement, it was going downhill. I could feel it all falling apart then. There was no doubt that he cared for us all. He just was not strong enough to fight the urges to get high. Being unable to fight the urge to get high is not a weakness. It is the individual's mental and physical reaction to the drugs. Each person has a different level of power to cope. For some, it is easier and more rewarding at the moment to just give in to the feeling.

I knew I could not stay. My heart was hurting now. Having secured a position with a non-profit, I was sent to Atlanta for training. My new boss booked a first-class seat for me. I had never flown before. I was told that he would be on the same flight and would hold my hand all the way. Not realizing that this was just a way to soothe my anxiety and get me on the plane, I nervously searched for my boss. I did not see him anywhere, and so I boarded the plane. Leaving on a Tuesday, I was scheduled to return on Friday.

The electric bill was due on Friday before seven o'clock. My flight was scheduled to land at five-fifteen on

Friday. The agreement was that my partner would pay thebill. Once I returned, I would be able to pay the rent as he had been paying all the bills until then. Arriving at the airport at six o'clock p.m. on Friday, my oldest daughter told me the electric power at our house was turned off. Tami had come to stay with her sister while I went to Atlanta.

Before the trip to Atlanta, I had been working at a convenience store. Hearing the news about the lack of electricity at home, I rushed to the store to get my paycheck. The plan was to cash it and get to the power company before it was closed for the weekend. The manager at the store cashed my check right there at the store. I did not make it to the power company on time. There would be no power until Monday morning, when the bill could be paid. The girls went home with my sister, and I stayed at the house to wait for my partner.

Pulling into the yard, my partner came walking around the side of the house. When asked about the light bill payment, he said there was not enough money to pay the bill. Reaching into his back pocket pulling out three envelopes, he started ranting and raving about being used. The letters were checks that included my subsistence allowance and gas mileage from the new job. Snatching the checks out of his hand, I refused to argue. Laying down, I eventually dropped asleep. My partner did not come home that night. My tears were of sadness, frustration, and betrayal. The power was turned back on that Monday morning two days later. That same evening, his oldest daughter and her son moved out of the house with us. The power was never restored to the relationship between my partner and me.

Drug addiction and infidelity reared their ugly head, twisting and consuming whatever love was between us. My partner provided a home, paid the bills, and continued to use drugs every day. He hid this from me for a time. Shortly after that, there was no hiding to get high. He started to bring the drugs into the house. Our twelve-year-old daughter was there. Returning from a training workshop earlier than expected one day, he was seen cooking out with his former girlfriend. Seeing this hurt a lot. Using the drugs was bad enough, but this disrespect was too much. To make matters worse, he was just down the street from our house.

Our daughter asked to spend the holidays in South Carolina with her sister; I agreed, so she was not there during this bad time. While Selena was with her sister for two weeks, I paid the deposit on our new apartment. We made the final move to the new apartment one week later. Each day her stomach was upset, and she did not seem to have any appetite.

She had come back from South Carolina pregnant. At fifteen, she did not know what to expect. It dawned on me when her sickly stomach would not go away. We had the talk about becoming a woman and where babies came from a couple of times prior. I did not know she was havingsex. She told me it was her first time.

Going into the house, everything that could fit into the car was packed up and moved that same day. The furniture will be moved the next week. This was only five months after moving into the house. As soon as our daughter returned, she and I moved into a two-bedroom apartment. The bills were paid with the subsistence allowance and for the second time in my life. I received foodstamps. The apartment was kept for six months and then another move.

This time we moved into a small two-bedroom house on the other side of town. There were still two months before the baby was due.

This soon-to-be new Mama only wanted to eat Captain D's. Every day it was the same thing. All friends and family knew what a tear-jerking call was for. It was a way to get Captain D's every day. The baby arrived July 12,

1995! He was such a beautiful baby. His mother named him, Jamarius Runyel Champaign. The name sounded regal to me. His tombstone reads "Once a prince now a king."

At fourteen months of age, Jamarius started to get sick. By this time, we had moved back to South Carolina. The first sign was a swollen foot that he favored when walking. Looking

Carefully at his foot, there was no sign of a splinter or injury. The swelling did not go down, and so he was taken to the emergency room. There was found to be some deficiency in the messenger DNA that could not direct nutrients to the cells. This disease is called mitochondrial disease. It only happens in one in one thousand children. This inability to feed the cells causes organ failure and, most times, cognitive mental loss. Blindness was a common side effect.

Jamarius was released from the hospital three months later with a traque and oxygen support. He had to have around-the-clock care from then on. The disease affected his heart the most. It did not affect his brain. If anything, he was a wise old man that accepted the hand dealt with him. At the age of eighteen months, he had the heart of an eighty-year-old man. The question might be "Why not get a heart transplant?" The heart was not the only organ failing. The kidneys and liver were also failing rapidly. All the immediate family members were trained to care for my Pookie. He had been my Pookie from the moment I saw him. A registered nurse came every night and watched over him while the family slept. The doctors gave us the devastating news that children with this disease rarely lived to the age of six years.

The leading cancer research centers had no possible cure on the horizon for children with mitochondrial disease at the time. Even St. Jude's Research Center had no course of treatment that was different from what was already implemented. The family continued to pray for a miracle of healing. None of us realized that Jamarius was the miracle in our lives. He was loaned to us for such a short time, but he positively impacted the life of everyone he met.

Mama returned to attending high school once her son was home again. "Nandi" was what he called me, his Granny. We would spend many hours together every day. The exploration of all things outside was crucial in teaching him. Watching ants was a favorite pastime. He always wanted to know where the ants were going and why they moved so fast. My attempts to answer these and so many other questions made this child even more curious. There was a fifteen-minute window that Pookie could be separated from his machines. This time is when we would take a short walk around the yard. Using a cane to walk, his Nandi (Me) moved slowly. My left hip had just been replaced a few days before he was hospitalized that first time. While walking one day, Pookie found a small tree limb and started using it as a cane the same way I did! He propped it up against the step to use the next time we went outside. His ability to remember facts and assorted other things amazed me and everybody he met.

Some days we would go fishing at secret spots that were claimed as ours. Whether we caught fish or not was important. Teaching Pookie how to fish was the true lesson. If luck shined on us, a meal was made from the catch of the day! Our riddle was "Catch 'em, clean 'em, cook 'em and eat 'em!" Pookie watched very closely how the fish were cleaned. If given a chance, he would be able to clean the fish! Eating the fish was the best part for both of us. The only thing was the fish had to have the bones picked out before Pookie could eat them. Fileting helped, but still, there were small bones to be found. Fried fish and homemade hash browns were his favorite meal. It was my favorite too. His Mom or Auntie often grew tired of looking for bones in the cooked fish. Pookie would be told that all the fish was gone. He would always ask to see if all the fish was really gone! My little man and me ate a lot of fish in his short lifetime.

A Headstart Program was implemented in the Elementary schools. A child that was potty trained could attend. My Pookie (Jamarius) was registered and attended until his passing. He excelled in school and was quite the artist. A nurse came each morning to accompany him to school. That very first day, a white medical transport van arrived to take Pookie to school. He was not happy. He had been looking forward to riding on the yellow school bus. After much persuasion, he agreed to ride the white van that first day. A few days later, a small yellow school bus came to take him to school. The school bus came each day until his last day of school.

The nurse came every night at eleven to monitor Jamarius breathing while the family slept. Even though the nurse was there, none of the family could rest completely during the night. Exhaustion demanded some real sleep periodically. The school was going well for Pookie, but his mama was struggling. Pookie brought home this artwork of coloring barnyard animals. He had colored so well and stayed within the lines. He had added his own animal at the bottom. It was a detailed picture of an ant. An ant he had studied in his backyard. It was a perfect likeness of an ant!

The school environment for mama was so different from her real life. Probably all she could think about was her sick baby. This was while her friends and classmates considered much less in their worlds. No one would be able to concentrate with this much to think about. It The decision was made to find a part-time job. The job was with the Department of Natural Resources. It lasted just a few months. The job was an as-needed position. Sometime later, Mama found another job with the Charleston Post and Courier. It was the job she held until her baby crossed over the back into the arms of God.

No matter what the predicted outcome with illnesses, no one can prepare to say goodbye to a loved one. Coming home on the bus one day, Pookie was lethargic. By late that evening, his TT had to administer CPR. He was having trouble catching his breath, even with oxygen support. It would be his last hospital stay. The liver and kidney failure, along with the congestive heart failure, was just too much.

He was so tired. This was the only time he showed any reaction to the pain. He hurt badly and was kept sedated. His Nandi could not fix this for him or make it better. The family was called to the hospital to say goodbye and did so on that night so many years ago. Just thinking of it even now crushes my heart until I can hardly see to keep typing. I did not question God; I just wanted him to be here with me for a while longer. Some might ask, "How much longer"? My answer, of course, would be forever.

My daughter was wrapped up in hurt and the loss of her baby. Then the anger set in. The disregard for her own safety was questioned during this tough time. She did not realize that the loss of her child was not some form of punishment. I am sure to her it felt that way. All of that pain overshadowed the love of our God. Our small family cried together a lot during this time.

We all cried individually as well. Hiding from each other sometimes, the tears continued to flow spontaneously at times. Well-meaning people would say things that are meant to soothe, but in reality, are just so many empty words. The grieving process is not a tailormade. The process is never-ending.

The grieving has stages of revelation. The prayer of serenity would fit this time quite well. The first shock, the anger, and the acceptance have a place too. There is no timeline. It can be so hard even with faith-based counseling.

The time to gather around bereaved families is after the homegoing services are done. This is the time to make a short phone call or a short visit. Just let the family know you are there if needed. Jamarius lives on inside all of us as we think of him with love. It must have just seemed like empty words to my daughter then as everyone tried to console her. There is no doubt in my mind that most of what was said was not heard. It is now twenty-three years later. She has been blessed with another son, soon to be twenty-one years old.

This new boy came bursting into the world on a hot June thirteenth, in the year two thousand. He is named Jaelen Kahlil Frazier, a millennium baby for sure. This is a very changed world than when his brother was here. There are some similarities. Both boys were born while mama lived with their Granny. Both boys were spoiled by their Aunt TT! History does repeat itself because, just as in the past, mama moved into her own place just before the baby reached two years of age.

Jamarius (Pookie) loved to do somersaults, and so does Jaelen. Pookie is doing them in heaven, and Moo (Jaelen) is still doing somersaults at twenty years old! There is no logical or comical reason these nicknames were picked. The names just seemed to fit lovingly. Jaelen skips as he is walking from time to time. I love to see my Moo or anyone skipping. This says to the world, "it's alright." It will make you smile. Like his brother Moo remembers odd facts and information. He knows a lot about Greek mythology, among other things.

Fast-forwarding a bit. My health started to change. Several surgeries were needed and performed. There were knee surgeries, complete hysterectomy, and gall bladder removal in eighteen months. The body was not able to repair itself, and weakness took over. The absence of an appetite was major. My oldest told me later that she knew something was horribly wrong when there was no seafood in my house. There was no fish in the freezer and no desire to eat any. No matter what was going on with my health, my appetite for fish had never left me. It is still my favorite food!

During this time, no matter what food was placed in front of me, I had no desire to eat it. To make matters worse, the removal of my gall bladder did not help the nauseous feeling. The small noninvasive wound was not healing properly. My daughter was so scared that my sister was asked to come to visit from Florida. The fear on my sister's face was scaring me. My sister stayed a week with us but could not get me to eat more than a few bites of anything.

While my sister was with us, she took me to a doctor's appointment. The doctor wanted to see the gallbladder wound. A couple of days later, my sister returned to her home in Florida. A few days after this doctor's visit, the surgeon saw me in his office. He told my daughter, TT, to take me straight to the emergency room for admission into the hospital. The doctors were waiting for me at the emergency room and went to work right away. The first step was to release some of the infectious fluid from around the surgical incision. My daughter, TT, came downstairs as soon as she got off work. TT worked at the same hospital where I was being seen in the emergency room. I was admitted some hours later that evening. I would not return home for nearly four months.

A team of doctors came in to see me the next morning. I was told that all the blood work was not in at that time, but it appeared that I had lymphoma. Lymphoma is a type of cancer that affects the lymph nodes. Whether it was Hodgkin's or Non-Hodgkin's lymphoma had not been determined. The last of the blood results came later that afternoon. The doctor returned to explain that he had ordered a biopsy. A biopsy is when a piece of the tissue is cut off and sent to the lab for analysis. A piece of the tissue from the lymph node at the side of my neck was removed and sent to the lab. The next morning the doctor told my daughter and me that I did have Non-Hodgkin's lymphoma cancer.

The team of oncologists explained to my daughter and me that a combination of drugs had been most effective in treating many cases of this type of cancer. The treatment was not always successful. The treatment was started that same day intravenously. The veins in my arms were not cooperating anymore, so my doctor ordered a direct line be placed in my neck. This direct line is called a pik-line. The weeks and days before hospitalization were filled with numerous tests that required blood. The veins in my arms had stopped cooperating. A catheter was also put in at the same time. I did not have enough strength to get out of the bed to go to the bathroom. It was only a short walk of four to five feet, but it seemed so far from where I lay in the bed!

Food was not unappealing; it was just not important enough during this time. The food service staff did an outstanding job of preparing and presenting the selections. I just could not eat it. I was losing weight fast. This lack of appetite started weeks before hospitalization. It caused much concern for my daughter. TT was used to my healthy appetite, especially when it came to seafood. Weeks went by, and there was no change in the desire to eat. The only thing that seemed necessary was crushed ice. The nurses and nurse's aides kept the little picture-filled throughout the day and night.

The first round of chemotherapy felt like being heated on the inside. It was explained to me that as the chemotherapy killed bad cells, some good cells would die too. Maybe that is what was going on inside my body. The fight between good and not so good was waging a war of survival. There were times a definitive winner was not clear. There was always a lingering taste of metal inside my mouth.

During this time, it did not occur to me that I may not go home at some point. The question for me was when. The accelerated regimen of chemotherapy was begun. The medicine kept my body heated, and the air conditioner in my room had to be low. Every visitor and every caregiver complained of how cold the room was. Each morning I would sip my tea from the breakfast tray and then eat ice the rest of the day. I still had no appetite.

Seven days passed without any change. I was still in the hospital, weak as a newborn, and still, there was no appetite for food. Looking back on this time, the days actually seemed to pass rather quickly. In March and April, I had been admitted to the hospital just rolled right on in with no fanfare. There were no April Fool's jokes or tricks. Visitors came and went regularly.

Friends and family stopped by, and the deacons from the church came at least once a week. The deacons would always pray with me and give communion once a month. A monetary gift was left each time. I often wondered why this was done. I brought this up to my brother and cousin one evening as they visited me. My cousin said, well, "you may want to send out for something."

My sense of humor was still quite active most days. When my hair was falling out in clumps, I laughed about it. Having had lots of hair for most of my life, this did not bother me. I never really learned how to style/fix hair. Losing all of it took care of that dilemma! Certainly, I learned some haircare skills over the years. Those skills were always trumped by being too hot all the time. My scalp would sweat first. So, you see, going to the hairdresser was wasting money. The lovely hairstyle would hold maybe three days. It would be back to pulling it all together in a ponytail after that. It was too hot for me to wear wigs except in the winter, and only then for a few short hours.

The entire month of April was filled with chemotherapy, blood tests, and no appetite. My doctor left the country for six weeks. I was cared for by his colleagues. One doctor came by to see me each day. The question was always, "How are you feeling today?" My answer was always the same, "I feel okay." He would ask me if I had eaten anything, I would tell him I had. Then he would lift the cover of my plate and confirm that I had eaten nothing. The doctor encouraged me to just eat a forkful of eggs each morning to get some protein. I agreed to try.

I was fed formula by IV and told to drink ensure a dietary supplement. The physical and occupational therapist visited me regularly. The weakness had increased. The therapist helped me to sit up on the side of the bed propped up. My stay at the hospital was now six weeks and counting. My family and church family continued to visit me and pray for me. My niece would get off work and rush down to the hospital to see me and lotion my legs and feet. The chemotherapy was killing the skin cells causing them to flake and fall off.

No mirrors were positioned so that I could see into them. The medicine made my hair fall out in big clumps. My brother and my cousin would call and stop in to see me regularly. Through all of this, my brain worked well, and my sense of humor was alive and well. Everybody looked so worried and scared as they visited with me. My sense of humor shocked most of them. They were seeing what I had not seen yet. I was a very sick person. I do not suppose anybody had thought I was cute before, but now I must have looked a hot mess! As sick as I was, I was not too sick to continue laughing and praying. I thanked God for all He had done in my life. I thanked Him for everything. He kept me. He keeps me still, even now.

The month of May cruised right on in without a splash. Mother's Day and my birthday were on the same Sunday that year. I would celebrate both in the hospital. A former cancer patient and friend stopped by that day with a red rose for all the mothers in the hospital. This lady was surprised to see me there. She told me that two years prior, she had been released from the hospital's cancer unit on this day! This was her way of showing gratefulness and giving back. I appreciated it so much.

Sometime during this illness, my children convinced me to let my grandson come to visit me. Jaelen was only two years old when I was admitted to the hospital for my extended stay.

My girls did not know if I was going to make it. My little grandson was just two years old. We had spent so much time together. I am sure he wondered where I was. So, I agreed that he could come to see me in the hospital. I had missed him so much while I was being treated at the hospital. One day, he came into the room with that big, beautiful smile and said "Granny!" His mama lifted him up to give me a hug. He was scrambling to get out of her arms and into the bed with me. Eventually, he was allowed to sort of lay on the side of me in the bed.

We both were so happy to see each other. When the time came for them to leave, he refused. He held onto the railings of the bed with all his strength. Once they were able to pry him loose, he said, "My Granny is coming home to her little house!" Just thinking of it makes me cry! Somehow, he knew I would be coming home! By the time

I saw him again; he had turned three years old. I was still inthe hospital.

Some family came up from Florida to see my girls and to uplift them. The family came to the hospital to see me. About this same time, my doctor returned to the United States. He told me that the chemotherapy was working. The treatments were continued intravenously. The physical therapist had stood me up at the bedside. My appetite had not returned, but I was not feeling so weak anymore.

God was bringing me up and out of this. He was working on the inside. I could feel Him doing it for me again. A few days later, I took a few steps to the foot of the bed and ate a piece of toast. I had already lost eighty pounds. So excited to be out of bed and take baby steps, I told my daughter TT that I was ready to go home. She just laughed. She said, "Lady, you cannot go home just yet!" I was crushed!

The doctors told me once I was released from the hospital, my next stop would be a rehabilitation facility. I told my daughter that the moment they sent me to rehab, Iwanted a Pizza Hut meat lover's individual pan pizza and a Nehi soda. My desire for food was back. The ambulance delivered me to the rehab center, and in my room was a personal pan pizza and several flavors of Nehi soda! In the drawer were grape, orange, strawberry, and peach-flavored sodas. There was also an Arizona tea in there. I still could not really enjoy this, but it lifted my spirits just to see it.

Finally, that evening I saw myself for the first time since cancer had crept into our lives. Man, was I shocked! After the shock came anger. Why did my children let my little grandson see me looking like this? When I asked them, they explained that they were not sure if he would ever get a chance to see me again. The next day I went to the beauty parlor downstairs. The white beautician fixed what hair I had left. It lasted for two days. A few days went by, and I had her cut it all off and taper it. In a week, my hair had started to pop out in straight white strands. The loss of hair did not bother me in the least. The master was delivering me from cancer, and losing my hair did not concern me.

The Mommy that filled the mother space in my life came to the hospital regularly to check on me. At this time, she was always using a walker and cane. Insisting that it was not necessary for her to take the long walk from the parking lot up to my room fell on deaf ears. Laying there in the hospital, I would look up, and there she would be. Her smile and her continued prayers helped me. The oldest of her biological daughters was in a different hospital during this same time period. This must have been exhausting for her at seventy years old. Still, she made time for me. Love and gratitude for her caring brought me to tears after each visit.

Several chemotherapy sessions followed my release from the hospital and rehab. Rehab trained my body to support itself again. All the muscles were targeted. The strength returned, and the daily workouts continued. The twenty-one days in the rehab facility passed slower than the three months in the hospital. Finally, I was released to go home with my daughter TT. There were more chemotherapy infusions administered at the hospital. The infusion takes several hours. In October of 2003, I was in remission. Hallelujah! I thank you, Lord, for saving me again!

The schedule to visit the oncologist (cancer specialist) would be farther apart. Once the scheduled appointments dropped to six months (twice a year), the primary care physician took care of me. My primary care physician is the doctor that initially scheduled the hematology work-up. He knew something was not right. The blood tests showed white blood cell levels so low it alarmed the doctors. Medicines prescribed to bring the levels up worked for a time. At the time of the gall bladder removal, the levels were extremely low again.

The primary care doctor had all the history of what had happened since the last visit to her office. Entering the examination room, the doctor commented that the patient looked wonderful and healthy. I was the patient. The doctor teased about the weak, sick teacher she had seen the year before. Unable to walk into her office, my children had used a wheelchair to bring me in that time. The doctor looked tired to me. Most doctors have long hours and do often look tired, but this was different.

Showing up for the next scheduled appointment with the primary care physician, I was notified that one of the partners would see me. Questions about my regular doctor's absence were answered with vague responses. Before my next scheduled visit, a card arrived informing me that my doctor had passed away! A call to the office assured me that the partners would continue to see me. This time I was told the doctor had died from cancer. Of course, I offered my condolences to the family.

Thankful, grateful, and humbled is what consumed me. Another chance had been granted to me to do whatever it was that the Master had for me to do. I had to spread the message of forgiveness for and deliverance from all things detrimental to spiritual growth. Being granted favor and undeserved kindness from God was not taken lightly. I was still here because He wanted me here. Thank you, Lord. My undying love and devotion will never stop. I know why our parents prayed so much for us. It was not a choice; they had to pray for us as the elders had prayed for them. We are the proof that prayer works!

The first time out in public after surviving cancer this time was at my cousin's retirement party. A wig was worn to this event. Family and friends were surprised and happy to see me there. Being alive and able to attend was a big deal for me. This cousin is one of the nicest people I know. He came to see me in the hospital regularly, and I wanted to celebrate his day with the family. As usual, it was a classy affair. I was so glad I made it. As soon the prayer was finished, a beautiful double rainbow appeared on the

Charleston Harbor! It was the first time I had seen a doublerainbow in my life. Our God is so amazing.

My grandson, Jaelen was separated from his mama and came to live with me permanently at the age of seven. Living in the same house where he spent his first years on earth was okay with him. He called it my "little house" once he and mama had moved into their townhouse. Even though he loved being with me, he missed his mama so much. The two of us cried and prayed a lot during this time of separation from his mama. Sometimes he would try to hide and cry, and so would I. Sometimes the answers to his questions did not seem to fit. I always relied on God to direct me. He did not direct me toward the negative things, but He was always there throughout the negative times. He gave me the strength to go on.

The things that soothe an adult spirit are not soothing to a young child. The Lord does not cause thingsto happen in our lives but will allow certain things to take place. That is when the old saying, "this lesson is a blessing," becomes crystal clear. Eventually, my Moo and me created our own language of communicating. "Deedle Deet" was a language only the two of us understood. Later on, in his teen years, he would be embarrassed using it. Later still, he would start talking to me in our special code whenever he felt like it. It does not matter if others are present or not. His maturing had crossed over being embarrassed and entered the special territory.

The return to substitute teaching was uneventful. Although wigs had been bought, they were rarely worn. Worrying about what the children would say made me nervous. I went back to work anyway. Surprisingly, it was the adults at the schools that stared too long at the dramatic weight loss and the bald head. The children related stories of family members that had cancer and were bald like me. These children were tickled that my flip phone worked when it rang out loud. They laughed so hard. In their eyes, I was stuck in the past no matter how "cool" I was perceived. I must have lost lots of "cool" points that day. The phone upgrade happened only when that flip phone refused to work properly anymore.

The major part of these years of teaching was spent in classrooms of special needs children. The achievements and milestones accomplished held so much more meaning for these children. The everyday commitment of assisting in reaching these goals was very satisfying. There was never a dull moment. The repetitiveness of the teachings is a tool to helping the children learn.

This repeating process reminds me of a young boy that could not tie his shoelaces. The laces would flap or drag. This child did not speak but used sign language to communicate. The history between us started when the child was six years old. Each day the shoelace practice board was used to encourage tying the laces. His mom decided to buy Velcro closure shoes. Surprisingly, each day the child would still get the practice board to try to master the skill. This same child moved on to middle school. Substituting at the middle school one day for a different class, he spotted me. He ran up to me excitedly, waving his hands and then pointing at his shoes. The laces were perfectly tied! He undid them and tied them again so that I could see that he had mastered this skill! A hug was my reward. My smile was big for the rest of the day.

Teaching children of all levels continued until my last semester in college. Always wanting to finish college, I went back to school at the ripe old age of sixty-two. My oldest daughter enrolled with me. The plan was for us to walk across the stage together to receive our bachelor's degrees. Injuries from a devastating car wreck prevented TT from going more than a few semesters. My eyes and heart were in it for the duration. The school accepted many of my college credits from forty-two years earlier. The dream of graduating was realized two years later. Being able to limp across the stage with the class of 2014 was a thrill. The date was January 15th, 2015. We marched on Dr. Martin Luther King Jr.'s birthday. It was the coldest day/night in Charleston in January in fifty years. My heart was warmed by the number of people that came out anyway to support their loved ones. My family was there with me.

A couple of months prior to graduation, I did not take any teaching positions. The school course requirements were just too much. I was tired. One professor required a twenty-page final paper! I registered for this class and my final class of Seniors Seminar. This course that required the twenty-page final paper was not mandatory. There were 21 students in the first class as we reviewed the syllabus. The grumbling continuedthroughout the day. At the next class meeting, there were only 11 of us left. Near the end of the class, the count was down to 9. Stubborn and curious, I stayed for the duration.

Completing twelve pages of the final paper, I patted myself on the back. My back was hurting so badly; I saved my writing on the flash drive I had bought and stood up to stretch. Most work was done at the public library down the street from the house. To my astonishment when I tried to return to the paper, there was nothing but blank pages. Motioning for the library clerk to come over, I could hardly breathe. She could not help me retrieve the paper, although it should have been stored in the computer for 24 hours. The tears started to trickle down my face then. The paper was due in 12 hours. How was this possible? Could it be recreated? Arthritis crippled my hands years earlier, so typing was a challenge. Remembering what was in those pages was not the problem; typing it was the problem.

Explaining this to my oldest daughter TT, she volunteered to type it for me. The professor was notified about what had happened and gave more time to submit the paper. Apparently, some other members of the class had issues as well and needed more time. The deadline set for me according to the syllabus was not unreasonable. While appreciating the extended due date for the paper, I wanted to be done with all school assignments. Almost at the finish line, I started to unravel. TT came over, sat down with me as the paper was recreated, and typed it all for me. Rushing to Fed Ex, the finished paper was uploaded to the professor on time. A few days later, the professor released the grades.

I received an A. In my discombobulation, I had used the first name of a past professor and the last name of the current professor! The professor laughed. Had I not done this, maybe I would have gotten an A+! I was very happy with my A and thanked the good Lord. A huge thanks to my first daughter, TT, for her fast-typing fingers!

Some friends and family questioned my return to school. I had already stopped working at any regular job for a long time. The answer was quite simple if not returning to get my degree I would still be sixty-four years old anyway. During this time, my daughters had started and stopped college a few times. My grandson was still in the house with me, trying to navigate the teen years. His confusion in an ever-changing world concerned me the most. I had been gifted with another grandson in 2005. The children must understand that education would help them to work smart and not just work hard all their lives. With no regrets, "it is true that hindsight is always perfect vision."

The newest addition to the family made his entrance with hardly a cry on January 29, 2005. However, this quietness would not last. Both grandfathers and the father of the new addition were named James. His mother named this boy James. He was a screamer. A screamer is a baby that cries even when they are fed, dry and healthy. The non-stop wailing continues through baby rockers, family singing, and walking around with the baby in your arms. Laying on granny's chest, next to her heart, helped sometimes. If this did not work and sleep was required, granny made sure the little one could not fall or get hurt in any way. Holding him gently to her chest as he screamed, she would go to sleep. As she woke up periodically, he would be fast asleep. Easing James onto his own blanket, both got a good nap. James Trenard Anthony referred to as JT, emerged from the screaming stage into a stage of independence. I affectionately call him Snook. The name stuck for me. It is very difficult for a new mother to get any quality downtime. Without help, this can be a terrible time for mom and baby. The only way to rest is the tried and proven system of sleeping when the baby sleeps. With all the things a new mom must navigate, is this even possible? Exhaustion from lack of sleep makes it possible. Factor in postpartum issues, and there is a recipe for chaos.

The much relied on "pacifier" was put to rest after many times of JT talking around it. Granny knew the time had come and placed it within sight and reach. The designated place was next to the bed on the nightstand. It was as if JT had waited for us to decide it was time to stop using the pacifier. There was not much fussing about it at all. He was a big boy now and did not need it anymore. There were all types of digital games to entertain a child, but Granny still believed the best fun was to go outside and enjoy the world. Raking and bagging leaves were one of our most favorite outside activities. The hard work made break times more enjoyable. The boys could identify all kinds of birds, insects, and other creatures living outside.

Both boys spent considerable time with Granny (Me) at my "little" house. There were some great movie times with popcorn and candy. The best times were spent outside. Just like the grandchildren before him, JT watched me hobble around using my cane. Once we were outside for a bit, he carefully chose his walking stick. He mimics my walking by limping and occasionally grunting, moving slowly from place to place. They got a lot of exercise because I could not get my balls if I were pitching. I could not get the balls if I were catching and missed. After so much fun, the boys would always try to bring their walking canes inside. Once the realization hit me that they had brought sticks into the house, I made them take them back outside. Most times, the sticks were placed right next to the door to be used again. My daughters thought the boys mimicking me was hilarious.

Soaring screaming hawks inhabited the area, and one old wise owl lived in the big tree in the backyard. The boys were interested in all things that moved. Grabbing some bug and bringing it to Granny was not unusual. It's as if the boys thought Granny had unlimited knowledge of many things. A detailed exact image of a soaring hawk was drawn by Jaelen one day. He was told to sign his name at the bottom, which he did. It was perfect. Jaelen took it to school the next morning without permission. He said he took it to show his art teacher. The drawing was never seen again. The boys learned so much from spending time outside. Random facts about many things just pour out of them.

During the pecan harvesting time, the boy's pent-up energy was put to good use in picking up pecans. The big old pecan tree was very old. Some say maybe a hundred or more years old. It produced the fat round paper shell variety that everyone craved. The first good, sustained wind of the season made the pecans drop to the ground. Every other year the harvest was so plentiful eating pecans would be enjoyed all year long. It also ensured the scrounging by neighbors for the good pecans. It is a very popular tree. The owner of the property always made cakes each holiday season using the nuts. The favorite way for us to enjoy the pecans was just to break the shell and eat the meat inside. A lot of cakes were made and given to loved ones a day or two before Christmas. Being included in the group to receive the cakes was an honor. Sadness took over when the little lady could no longer make those cakes. Her health issues made it impossible to continue the hard love work required to make those cakes. Everyone will always remember the smooth sweet, nutty flavor of the cakes. It was better than any so-called fruit cake.

Grandson number three, JT(Snook), grew up so fast. It seems the years started to speed past. One day he was the "screamer." then, he was graduating from kindergarten. A lot happened in-between times. Both boys became percussionists and wrestlers for a time. Both played in basketball youth leagues. JT is a freshman and percussionist in his high school band. Jaelen is almost twenty-one years old, still unsure which direction to go. He will be alright, though.

Some folks never figure out which way to go. He must remember who our true Father is and honor Him. Our Lord and Savior want us to prosper and live in His abundance. Jaelen is young, smart, talented, and undisciplined. Living in a world with access to the entire world with the touch of a finger can be overwhelming. This navigation requires focusing, and it is harder for some than for others. A valuable lesson to be learned is, God is not going to give you more until you show you can handle what has been given.

Brutal honesty is painful. Fifty years ago, at twenty, the mirror image of myself was Jaelen. I do not mean disrespecting elders. What I mean is living life for the moment. Let us be clear; no twenty-year-old thinks their time will be up in an instant. If the thought does cross the mind, the next thought is probably "live until you die." However, one might believe that young people should wake up in these trying times. In our twenties and thirties, we did not. Our generation did fight together for justice, civil rights, and equality under the law. The new generation attempts to live in a separate world. A world that is even separate from each other.

This generation of young people has seen death up close and personal. Saying goodbye to friends and family because of violence, illness, and unexplained causes has shaken them up. It is mind-boggling how often these children said farewell to loved ones in just the past year. Before one can wrap the brain around losing one, another has crossed over. Regardless of the reason for the loss, the heart and mind are in turmoil. Many of these children rely on drugs to soothe the hurt left behind. Others retreat into themselves as they block out any and everybody. It is a sad state that regards sharing or showing any love or compassion as a negative emotion. I guess the reasoning is that if nothing is felt, there is no pain. Then there is the stigma of admitting help is needed to come through this trauma. It is just as hard for girls as for boys. I thank God and His precious love for being constantly in their lives.

There were certainly some losses growing up. There is no need to list them all here, but some must be mentioned.

The first experience of death involving children known to us happened in the second grade. A classmate drowned while on a fishing trip with his dad. In those times, the community, it seemed, functioned as a single entity. The news spread swiftly all over.

The family and others decided this would be a good time to have the deceased classmates assigned to assist in the homegoing celebration! A seven-year-old standing next to a casket reciting some poem, singing, or reading scripture was terrifying. The smell of those funeral flowers was nauseating. In those days, the beautiful gladiola flower was in abundance as it was less expensive. The smell would linger for days in the church. It was very nauseating, coupled with the smell of roses, cologne, and perfume.

There were no computerized games to divert thefocus of a child. The nightmares would eventually come andlast. Almost a year later, a classmate and his first cousin drowned in this same creek on the outskirts of town. Our class was in the third grade now. The oldest of these victims was our classmate. He had only moved to our town six months prior to his death. There was a blanket of sadness that engulfed us. It was heavy enough that one could almost imagine lifting it off and folding it up to be stored someplace else.

Children were not encouraged to express their feelings as is practiced today. To suffer in silence was the order of the day. Each child that attended the same school must have struggled with death and dying. All of us, not yet recovered from the loss of our friend and classmate in the second grade had more to live with. When the subject of death came up at such a young age, there was no way to express our feelings. It was as though the deceased never lived. It is certain that many go back in their minds to these times so many years ago.

One more devastating loss happened as our class entered the sixth grade. The torture and murder of an older female teen from our neighborhood froze us with fear. There was only one high school for Black children in our county. High school students had to board the bus in our area at 5:45 in the morning. This child was dragged from the bus stop, attacked, and killed one cold morning. As much as our parents tried to shelter us from evil, bits and pieces of what happened were found out. The killer was found the same day, but the fear had seeped into our minds already. Could this happen to us when it was our time to go to high school in a couple of years?

These life-altering catastrophes are not minimized. The children today deal with more of the same and an added menace. The previous generation and the one immediately prior live by a code of callous killing. Besides the ill-treatment of the entire race, it is a constant killing of each other of the same race. Not pretending to understand it; the logic is flawed.

The scales are tipped for disaster because of fear. There has always been illegal use and profit from selling drugs. Gangs and gambling have been around. The ones that have chosen this lifestyle exist by a different code.

These people exist. They are not living at all. Wondering when the body in the street might be theirs is not living. A contender is already prepping for the takeover.

Games that have nothing to do with reality are played for hours every day. It became more important to reach another level of playing skill than to find and keep a job. Some of the games show you how to commit murder. The worldwide web allows access to any and everything one might imagine. Information on making ice cream and building a gun silencer is available to anyone that has just basic computer skills.

No cliches need to be quoted here. However, there are a few that come to mind. This living testimony is real. The Master saved me despite myself. He gathered me in His loving arms and brought me to this place of thankfulness, gratitude, and praise. A sick body, a sick mind, and a weak spirit did not stop His love for me. I just had to hold on. Everyone must hold on. Change is going tohappen whether it is orchestrated by us or allowed by the Lord. The fact is there is not one single thing that can be accomplished alone. There is nothing we can do without God. There could be no walking, talking, eating, sleeping, or waking up without Him holding our hand. So, if God is all you have, then you have everything you need. I know Ido. Thank you Lord, for everything.

• • •